Published in Great Britain by **Cassell**
Villiers House, 41/47 Strand, London WC2N 5JE

Published in the United States of America by **Abingdon Press**
201 Eighth Avenue South, PO Box 801, Nashville, Tennessee 37202

Published in Australia by **The Joint Board of Christian Education**,
10 Queen Street, Melbourne, Victoria 3000

Adapted from **La Bible** by Blandine Marchon, published by Editions du Centurion, Paris

English-language edition first published 1992

British Library Cataloguing-in-Publication Data
A catalogue record for this book is available from the British Library.

Library of Congress Cataloging-in-Publication Data
Available from the Library of Congress.

ISBN 0-304-32633-X (Cassell)
    0-687-03115-X (Abingdon)
    0-85819-842-8 (JBCE, Australia)

Printed and bound in France by Bayard Presse

THE Bible

THE GREATEST STORIES

Written by Blandine Marchon

Illustrated by Claude and Denise Millet

CASSELL

ABINGDON

JOINT BOARD OF CHRISTIAN EDUCATION

Contents

The Old Testament

In the beginning   10
Genesis chapter 1;
chapter 2, verses 1 to 4

The wonderful garden   14
Genesis chapter 2, verses 4 to 24

Tempted by the serpent   15
Genesis 2, verse 25;
chapter 3 verses 1 to 7

Driven out of the garden   16
Genesis chapter 3, verses 8 to 23

Cain kills his brother   17
Genesis chapter 4, verses 1 to 15

Saved from the flood   18
Genesis chapters 6 to 9

The giant tower of Babel   22
Genesis chapter 11, verses 1 to 9

God calls Abraham   23
Genesis chapter 12, verses 1 to 7;
chapter 15, verses 2 to 6

A mysterious visit   24
Genesis chapter 18, verses 1 to 15

Abraham sacrifices his son Isaac   26
Genesis chapter 22, verses 1 to 13

Joseph betrayed by his brothers   27
Genesis chapter 37, verses 1 to 34

Joseph in prison   29
Genesis chapters 39 and 40

Pharaoh's chief minister   30
Genesis chapter 41, verses 1 to 41

The brothers face to face   31
Genesis chapters 41 to 44

The family is together again   34
Genesis chapters 45 to 49

Slaves in Egypt   35
Exodus chapter 1, verses 8 to 22

A baby saved from the water   36
Exodus chapter 2, verses 1 to 10

The burning bush   37
Exodus chapter 2, verses 11 to 15;
chapter 3, verses 1 to 14

Panic in Egypt   38
Exodus chapters 7 to 10

The great escape   41
Exodus chapter 12

Crossing the sea   42
Exodus chapter 14

Hungry in the desert   44
Exodus chapter 16, verses 1 to 15

The ten commandments   45
Exodus chapters 19, 20 and 24

The golden calf   46
Exodus chapter 32, verses 1 to 34

The ark of the covenant   48
Exodus chapter 33, verses 18 to 23;
chapter 40, verses 16 to 38

The death of Moses   49
Deuteronomy chapter 34

The promised land at last   50
Joshua chapter 3, verses 7 to 17

The siege of Jericho   52
Joshua chapter 6, verses 1 to 20

The choice of God   54
Joshua chapter 24, verses 1 to 29

The exploits of Samson   55
Judges chapters 13 to 16

Samuel, the child God called   57
1 Samuel chapter 3

Saul, the first king of Israel   58
1 Samuel chapters 8, 9, 10 and 15

David, the shepherd who became king   59
1 Samuel chapter 16, verses 1 to 13

David fights the giant   60
1 Samuel chapter 17, verses 1 to 51

Saul hunts for David   62
1 Samuel chapter 24, verses 3 to 21

David takes over Jerusalem   64
2 Samuel chapter 5, verses 1 to 9;
chapter 6, verses 17 to 19

A new promise from God   65
2 Samuel chapter 7, verses 1 to 17

King Solomon and the stolen baby   66
1 Kings chapter 3, verses 16 to 28

The most beautiful temple in the world   67
1 Kings chapter 5, verses 16 to 32;
chapter 6

Jerusalem on fire   68
2 Kings chapter 24, verses 8 to 17;
chapter 25, verses 1 to 12

Freed from exile!   69
Ezra chapters 1 to 6

Judith, the courageous widow   70
Judith chapters 7 to 16

Esther the brave   72
Book of Esther

Under foreign occupation   74
1 Maccabees

The sufferings of Job   76
Book of Job

God is like a potter   78
Jeremiah chapter 18, verses 1 to 10

The song of the three children in the fire   79
Daniel chapter 3, verses 14 to 28

Daniel in the lions' den   80
Daniel chapter 6, verses 12 to 28

Jonah runs away from God   82
Book of Jonah

The one who will come   85
Isaiah chapter 11, verses 1 to 9

The New Testament

The message to Mary 88
Luke chapter 1, verses 26 to 38
The amazing birth of Jesus 89
Luke chapter 2, verses 1 to 19
The wise men and the star 91
Matthew chapter 2, verses 1 to 12
Jesus is lost 92
Luke chapter 2, verses 41 to 52
The baptism of Jesus 93
Mark chapter 1, verses 4 to 13
Fishers of men and women 94
Mark chapter 1, verses 16 to 20
The wedding at Cana 96
John chapter 2, verses 1 to 11
A paralysed man is cured 97
Mark chapter 2, verses 1 to 12
The secret of happiness 98
Matthew chapter 5, verses 1 to 12
Words of life 99
Matthew chapter 6, verses 9 to 13; chapter 22, verses 35 to 40
The story of the sower 100
Matthew chapter 13, verses 1 to 9
The treasure and the pearl 101
Matthew chapter 13, verses 44 to 46
The rich young man 102
Matthew chapter 19, verses 16 to 22
Living water 103
John chapter 4, verses 1 to 24
The Lord of the sea 104
Mark chapter 4, verses 35 to 41
Feeding the thousands 105
Mark chapter 6, verses 30 to 44
Who is Jesus? 107
Mark chapter 8, verses 27 to 33
The transfiguration of Jesus 108
Mark chapter 9, verses 2 to 8
Jesus and the children 109
Mark chapter 10, verses 13 to 16
The good Samaritan 110
Luke chapter 10, verses 29 to 37
The lost sheep 111
Luke chapter 15, verses 1 to 7
The prodigal son 112
Luke chapter 15, verses 11 to 32
The little man in the tree 114
Luke chapter 19, verses 1 to 10
Blind Bartimaeus 115
Mark chapter 10, verses 46 to 52
Triumph in Jerusalem 116
Mark chapter 11, verses 1 to 11
Panic in the temple 118
Mark chapter 11, verses 15 to 18

A woman condemned to death 120
John chapter 8, verses 3 to 11
Lazarus comes back to life 121
John chapter 11, verses 1 to 53
Judas betrays Jesus 123
Mark chapter 14, verses 1 to 2, and 10 to 11
The last supper 124
Mark chapter 14, verses 12 to 31
Arrested at night 126
Mark chapter 14, verses 32 to 50
Peter's denial 127
John chapter 18, verses 13 to 27
Jesus is questioned 128
John chapter 18, verses 28 to 40
Sentenced to be crucified 129
John chapter 19, verses 1 to 16
Jesus is crucified 130
John chapter 19, verses 17 to 41
Jesus is alive! 132
John chapter 20, verses 1 to 18
Thomas asks for proof 134
John chapter 20, verses 19 to 29
On the road to Emmaus 135
Luke chapter 24, verses 13 to 35
Jesus goes to his Father 137
Acts of the Apostles chapter 1, verses 4 to 11
The wind of Pentecost 138
Acts of the Apostles chapter 2, verses 1 to 41
Brothers and sisters 140
Acts of the Apostles chapter 2, verses 42 to 47
Two apostles arrested in the temple 141
Acts of the Apostles chapter 3; chapter 4, verses 1 to 21
Stephen is stoned 142
Acts of the Apostles chapter 6, verses 8 to 15; chapter 7
Paul's experience on the road to Damascus 144
Acts of the Apostles chapter 9, verses 1 to 20
Paul's travels for God 146
Acts of the Apostles chapters 13 to 28
If I have no love 148
1 Corinthians chapter 13, verses 1 to 13

Six questions about the Bible 150

Index 152

THE OLD TESTAMENT

In the beginning ...

In the beginning God created heaven and earth.
The earth was formless and empty and in complete
darkness. The breath of God wandered over the
waters.

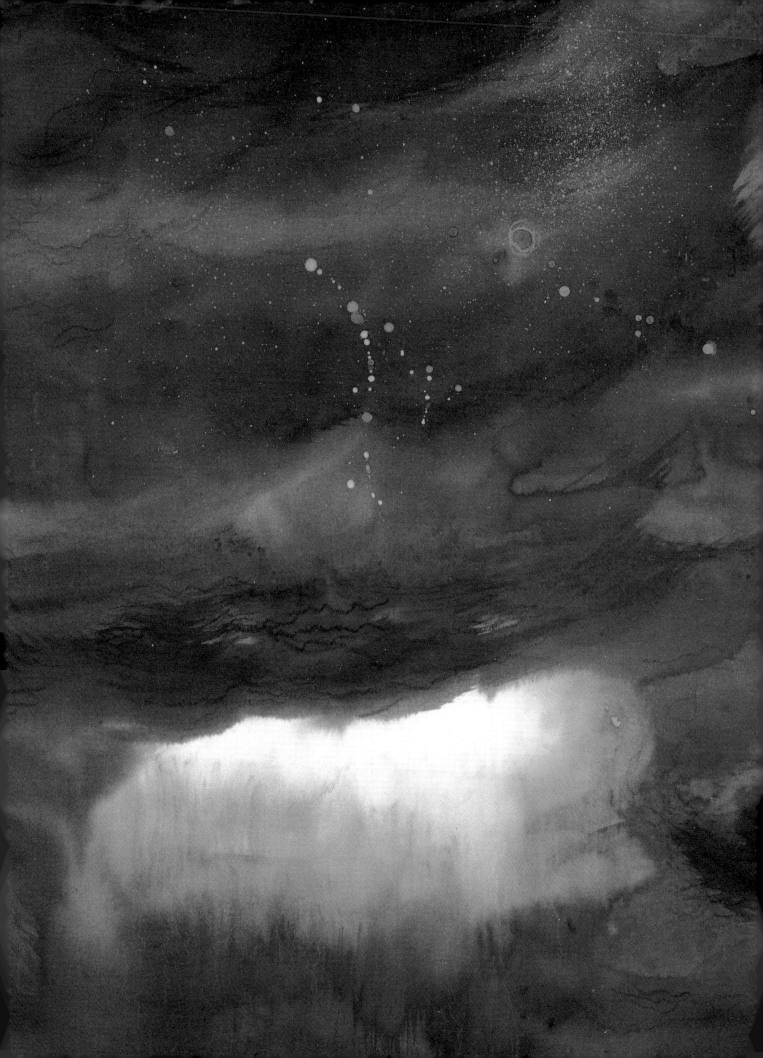

Does the Bible tell exactly how the world was made?

The purpose of the Bible stories of creation is to tell that God made the world. The Bible shows in a poetic way that through God's will the world came into being, that the world is good, and that human beings have responsibility for the world. The creation story was written about 2,500 years ago; it is not meant to be a scientific explanation of how the universe came to be.

On the first day God said:

"Let there be light!"

And there was light. God saw that the light was good and God separated the light from the darkness. God called the light "day" and the darkness "night".

On the second day God said:

"Let there be a space between the waters!"

And this came to be. God called the space between the waters above and the waters below "sky".

On the third day God said:

"Let the waters below get together in one place so that dry land can appear."

This happened, and God called the land "earth" and the waters "sea". And God saw that it was good.

And God said:

"Let the earth be covered with green, with plants and trees and their seeds and fruits."

This came to be, and God saw that it was good.

On the fourth day God said:

"Let there be lights in the sky to separate day and night. Let them show the feasts and the seasons, the days and the years, and let them give light to the earth."

This came to be. God made two great lights for the earth: the sun by day and the moon by night. He also made the stars. And God saw that it was good.

On the fifth day God said:

"Let the waters be full of living creatures and let birds fly in the air."

God made all the animals that come and go in the water, and every kind of bird. God saw that it was good. God blessed them and said:

"Multiply yourselves in the sky and in the sea."

On the sixth day God said:

"Let the earth bring forth many different animals: little ones and big ones, wild and tame, two-, four- and six-legged creatures."

This happened. And God saw that it was good. Finally God said:

"Let us make human beings in our own image, like us. Let them be responsible for all the animals."

God made human beings in the image of God, male and female; then God blessed them:

"Have children, increase your numbers, fill the earth and be in charge of it. Eat the seeds and fruits, and let the animals eat the grass."

This was what happened. God saw that everything created was very good.

The seventh day came. God had finished the work, and rested. God blessed this day and made it a special day dedicated to God.

Why does the Bible say that God created the world in seven days?

For those who wrote down the creation story, the Sabbath day was a gift from God, a sacred day dedicated to God, when neither people nor animals had to work. They believed that the Sabbath began with God's creation of the world. God created the world in six days, and rested on the seventh, making that day holy.

From the Book of Genesis, chapter 1, and chapter 2, verses 1 to 4.

The wonderful garden

Isn't there an apple in the story?

No, that was a mistake made by people who read the Bible in Latin. "Malum" in Latin means "evil" and "apple". So the evil fruit was called an apple!

When God made heaven and earth, there were no trees, no plants and no human beings. God took some clay from the earth and shaped a man. God breathed in his nostrils and the man came to life. God made a wonderful garden: in the centre he put the tree of life, and the tree of the knowledge of good and evil. He gave this garden to man to take care of, but said to him:

"You may eat the fruit of all the trees in the garden, except the tree of the knowledge of good and evil. If you eat from this tree you will die."

Then God said:

"It is not good that the man should be alone."

So from clay he modelled all the animals and brought them to the man. And the man gave a name to each animal, but he still had no one who was an equal and a companion. So God put the man to sleep, and took some flesh from his side and made a woman. He brought her to the man, and the man said:

"She is really the same flesh as me. She will be my companion. Her name is woman."

From that time on, men and women would leave their parents and love each other. Husbands and wives would be one.

From the Book of Genesis, chapter 2, verses 4 to 24.

Tempted by the serpent

The man and woman were naked and helpless before God, but they were not ashamed. The serpent, the most wicked of the animals, asked the woman:

"Did God tell you not to eat the fruits in the garden?"

She replied:

"We can eat the fruit from all the trees, except the tree in the middle of the garden. If we do, we shall die."

The serpent said:

"No, you won't die! God knows very well that if you eat it, you will know happiness and pain, and so you will be like gods."

The woman was drawn towards the tree. She picked one of its fruits, took a bite, and gave it to the man, who ate some too. Suddenly they realized their weakness and nakedness: they were embarrassed. They made themselves clothes of fig leaves.

From the Book of Genesis, chapter 2, verse 25 to chapter 3, verse 7.

Why did God say they should not eat the fruit?

The fruits of this tree represented the knowledge of happiness and pain. Human beings by eating them would have the same knowledge as God. And so they would want to go their own way, not God's way. God knew that this would make the world unhappy.

Driven out of the garden

The man and the woman heard God coming and hid. God called the man:

"Where are you?"

The man answered:

"I was ashamed of being naked, so I hid."

"Who told you that you were naked? Have you eaten the fruit from the forbidden tree?"

"My friend: she gave it to me and I ate it."

God said to the woman:

"Why did you do this?"

The woman replied:

"The serpent tempted me, and I ate it!"

God said to the serpent:

"You will be an animal that everybody hates."

God said to the woman:

"You will suffer too, and your relationship with your husband will be full of problems!"

Then God said to the man:

"You will have to work hard to find food, then you will die and be buried in the ground."

God made them clothes from animals' skins, and drove them out of the garden.

From the Book of Genesis,
chapter 3, verses 8 to 23.

Cain kills his brother

The man, Adam, and the woman, Eve, had children.
The eldest, Cain, grew crops. The second, Abel, was a
shepherd. Cain and Abel offered sacrifices to God:
Cain offered things he had grown, and Abel offered
the first-born lambs from his flock. God accepted
Abel's offering but not Cain's. Cain was furious, and
asked Abel to go out into the fields with him, and
killed him. Then he heard God speaking to him, and
saying:

"Cain, where is your brother Abel?"

"I don't know," said Cain. "Am I my brother's
keeper?"

"What have you done? You've killed him!" said God.
"You will suffer for this. You will work on the land,
but nothing will grow for you. Get out!"

"My punishment is too heavy, Lord," pleaded Cain.
"If you send me away someone will kill me."

"If anyone kills you, they will be punished," said
God.

And God put a sign on Cain so that no one would
dare to kill him.

From the Book of Genesis,
chapter 4, verses 1 to 15.

***Why did God refuse
Cain's offering?***

*The Bible does not
say. But other parts
of the Bible tell
us that what God
wants is the offering
of a good heart.
Perhaps that was
what Cain did not
give?*

Saved from the flood

Are there other ancient records of the flood?

Babylonian poetry and stories tell of great flood. Experts in ancient history have evidence of huge floods, but they have found no traces of a flood which could have destroyed the whole world. The flood story is intended to show Noah's faithfulness and God's promise not to destroy the whole world.

After some time had passed, God was sad to see that human beings were wicked, and all their thoughts were evil. God thought:

"I am sorry I created human beings and animals; I will wipe them out from the face of the earth."

But God rescued a man called Noah.

God said to him:

"Build an ark, and get into it with your whole family, because you are the only one who is good and just. Take two of every sort of animal, to save them from dying out. In seven days' time it will pour with rain for forty days until everything I have created is destroyed."

Noah did all that God had commanded. Seven days later the rain flooded the earth. All signs of life disappeared. Only Noah and the people and animals he had taken into the ark were left. After forty days, Noah sent out a crow, but the earth was still under water and the crow returned.

Later Noah sent out a dove, but she came back too.
He waited another week and sent her out again.
Towards evening, she came back with a young shoot
from an olive tree in her beak. So Noah understood
that the waters were already subsiding. A week later
he sent the dove out again. This time she did not
return. So Noah came out of the ark and offered
thanks to God. God was pleased, and said:
   "I shall never again destroy the earth because of
human wickedness. Even if humans are wicked, I shall
not destroy all life. As long as the earth endures, the
seasons of sowing and harvest will come and go, heat
and cold, summer and winter, day and night will
never cease."

God said to Noah and his children:

"Today I will make a covenant with you, and with all who come after you, and with all the living creatures who live around you. Here is the sign of the covenant between me and the earth: I will put my rainbow in the clouds. When the clouds gather over the earth and when I see the rainbow in the clouds, I shall remember my covenant and my promise to all living creatures and there will be no more floods."

From the Book of Genesis, chapters 6 to 9.

Why did God destroy the world he had made?

It was the wickedness of human beings that destroyed the world. When the flood ended God promised never to allow this to happen again. This is a way of showing in a story how God prefers to forgive, rather than to punish: and how God made a promise to the human race for ever.

The giant tower of Babel

Why did God confuse human language?

Those who wrote this story were simply trying to make this point: when people build a world without God, their pride divides them against each other. It seems that God wanted the difference in their languages to show their lack of unity.

There were more and more human beings. At that time everybody spoke the same language. People had travelled towards the east and found a great plain and settled in it. They said to each other:

"Let's make bricks and build a city and a huge tower right up to the sky. We'll be able to live together and we'll all be famous."

God saw the city and the tower the people had built. God thought:

"Human beings are getting together in cities and working together to make themselves more and more proud and important. If this goes on, they will think they can do anything."

So God made them all speak different languages so they could not understand each other any more. So they stopped building the tower and all went off to live in different parts of the earth.

From the Book of Genesis, chapter 11, verses 1 to 9.

God calls Abraham

MEDITERRANEAN SEA

CANAAN

Haran

Nineveh

Tigris

Euphrates

Babylon

Shechem
Mamre
Beersheba

Ur

To follow Abraham

Abraham was one of Noah's descendants. One day God called him and said:

"Leave your country and your family and your parents' house, and go to a country I will show you. I shall make you into a great nation; I shall bless you and make your name great. All the peoples on earth will be blessed through you."

Abraham left as God had told him. He arrived in Canaan and crossed it as far as the sacred oak of Moreh, at Shechem. There God appeared to him and said:

"This is the land I am giving you for your descendants."

Abraham replied:

"Lord God, you have not given me any children. When I die, all I have will be inherited by a servant born in my house."

"No," said the Lord, "you will have a son. Look up at the sky and count the stars if you can. Your family will be as many as the stars."

Abraham had faith in God. That is why the Lord found him to be just.

From the Book of Genesis,
chapter 12, verses 1 to 7, and
chapter 15, verses 2 to 6.

A mysterious visit

Who visited Abraham: God, or three men?

The story makes clear that it was God, but God appeared in the form of three strange visitors. This is how the story-teller shows us that God's action is always unexpected.

One day when Abraham was at Mamre, sitting in the shade of the oak trees, God appeared in front of his tent: what Abraham saw was three strangers. When he saw them Abraham bowed down and said:

"Lord, you have come near me, stay with me please. Rest here; I invite you to supper. Have some rest before you go further."

The strangers said:

"That's good."

So Abraham ran to ask Sarah, his wife, to make some cakes and roast a calf. He also offered them white cheese and milk. He stood beside them and watched them eat.

They asked Abraham:

"Where is Sarah, your wife?"

Abraham replied:

"In the tent."

One of the strangers said:

"I will come back in a year's time, and by then Sarah will have a son."

Sarah had heard what the stranger said, and as she was very old, she started to laugh quietly.

But God said to Abraham:

"Why did Sarah laugh? Why does she not believe what I have told you? Cannot God do what God wills? I shall return in a year's time and Sarah will have a son."

Sarah was frightened, and said:

"I didn't laugh!"

But God said: "Yes, you did laugh."

As God had promised, Sarah had a baby boy one year later. Abraham called him Isaac, which means "child of laughter".

From the Book of Genesis,
chapter 18, verses 1 to 15.

Abraham sacrifices
his son Isaac

Does God ask for human sacrifices?

In those days human sacrifices were quite common. This story is told to show us that God asks humans to trust him, but God does not want human sacrifices.

Isaac had grown. And it was time for God to test Abraham's obedience. He called him:

"Abraham, take your only son Isaac, whom you love. offer him to me as a sacrifice on the mountain which I will show you."

Abraham got up early, loaded wood for the sacrifice onto his donkey and set off with his son.

Three days later, they came to the mountain. Abraham had fire, a knife and the wood for the fire, which Isaac was carrying. Isaac asked him:

"Father, I can see the fire and the wood, but where is the lamb for the sacrifice?"

"The lamb? God will provide a lamb."

Abraham built an altar, put the wood on it and tied Isaac up and put him on top. He took the knife to kill him for the sacrifice. But suddenly he heard a voice from heaven:

"Abraham, Abraham, do not kill the child. I can see now how much you trust me, since you are even willing to give me your son."

Abraham then saw that a ram was caught by its horns in a bush. He sacrificed the ram to God in place of Isaac, his son.

From the Book of Genesis,
chapter 22, verses 1 to 13.

Joseph betrayed by his brothers

Isaac's son, Jacob, lived in the land of Canaan. He had twelve sons, but Joseph was the one he loved best. For Joseph's seventeenth birthday Jacob gave him a wonderful coat. His brothers were very jealous and hated him. But Joseph did not realize this, and he did not take care not to annoy them. One day he told his father and brothers about a dream he had had:

"The sun, the moon and eleven stars bowed down to me."

His father rebuked him:

"What sort of dream is this? Are you saying we will all have to bow down to you one day?"

But Jacob often thought about Joseph's dream. One day he sent Joseph out to fetch his brothers home: they had gone out to look after the flocks.

They saw him coming in the distance and they said among themselves:

"Ah, here comes the dreamer! Let's kill him. We can say a wild animal got him."

One of them, Reuben, wanted to save his brother. He said:

"Don't let's kill him. Let's just put him down a well." He thought he would come back later and rescue Joseph. Joseph's brothers grabbed Joseph, took his lovely coat, and threw him down a dry well.

Could people be bought and sold in those days?

Yes. You could buy or exchange men, women and children as slaves, to be servants or entertainers.

Seeing a caravan of merchants on their way to Egypt they pulled Joseph out of the well and sold him. Then they killed a kid, and dipped Joseph's coat in the blood. They gave it to their father. When he saw the coat he recognized it and was convinced Joseph was dead. He cried for a long time.

From the Book of Genesis,
chapter 37, verses 1 to 34.

Joseph in prison

The merchants sold Joseph to Potiphar, the Adviser to Pharaoh, King of Egypt, and Commander of the Royal Guard. God was with Joseph and helped him, and Joseph did well in all his work. Potiphar was so pleased with him that he asked him to look after his own household and all his possessions. Joseph did this so well that Potiphar made him very rich.

But Potiphar's wife had noticed Joseph. One day she said to him:

"Come to bed with me."

"Never," said Joseph, "my master trusts me, and I don't want to hurt him or to offend God."

But she went on asking him every day. One day when she was alone, she caught Joseph by the coat and whispered:

"Come with me!"

But Joseph pushed her away and ran off, leaving his coat in her hands. When Potiphar came in, she said to him:

"That slave you brought here wanted to go to bed with me! I shouted, and he ran away, leaving his coat!"

Potiphar was very angry with Joseph and threw him in prison. While he was there, Joseph was still helped by God. The chief guard became his friend and put him in charge of the work the prisoners were doing. In prison Joseph met Pharaoh's wine steward and his chief baker, who had been sent to prison for bad work.

One night, each of them had a dream, and Joseph was able to explain the meaning of their dreams. What Joseph prophesied came true: one was hanged and the other set free.

From the Book of Genesis,
chapters 39 and 40.

What was a Pharaoh?

The kings of Egypt in ancient times were called Pharaoh. They ruled over a very rich country, watered by the river Nile.

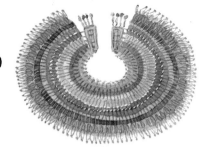

Pharaoh's chief minister

Why is there so much about dreams in the Bible?

The Jews believed that certain dreams were very important. They believed that God spoke through these dreams in a mysterious way.

Two years later, Pharaoh had a dream: he saw seven fat cows coming out of the Nile, and then seven thin cows came out and ate them up.

No one could explain the meaning of this dream, but the wine steward remembered Joseph and told Pharaoh about him. Pharaoh immediately sent for Joseph from the prison and asked him:

"Is it true that you can interpret dreams?"

"I can't interpret them by myself," said Joseph, "only with God's help."

So Pharaoh told him his dream and Joseph explained its meaning:

"God wanted to warn you. The fat cows symbolize seven years of rich harvests. The thin cows symbolize seven years of famine which will come after them."

Then he added:

"You need to find a wise person who will build up big reserves of food during the rich years, and will let people have the food during the bad years. That way, Egypt will avoid famine."

Pharaoh was very impressed. "Since God is with you," he said, "no one could be wiser than you are. You must be my chief minister and govern Egypt."

From the Book of Genesis,
chapter 41, verses 1 to 41.

The brothers face to face

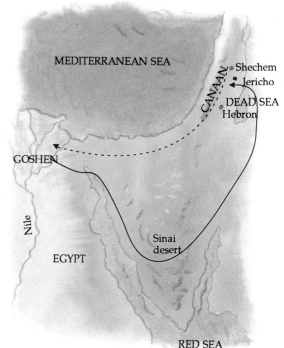

The seven years of good harvests began: Joseph was able to put aside huge corn reserves. Then the famine started. So Joseph was able to sell corn to the Egyptians.

In the land of Canaan where Joseph's family were still living, there was also a famine. Jacob sent Joseph's ten older brothers to buy corn in Egypt, but he kept Benjamin, the youngest, safe at home.

Joseph was also able to sell corn to foreigners. He recognized his brothers when they came, but they did not recognize him. Joseph spoke harshly to them:

"What do you want?" he asked.

"We've come from Canaan to buy corn."

"That's not true," he said, "you're spies."

"No, we're not. Our old father sent us here, and kept our youngest brother at home."

"To see whether you are telling the truth I'll keep one of you in prison, and you can bring back your youngest brother," said Joseph.

- - - - Route of Joseph and his brothers to Egypt

———— Probable route of the Exodus

They agreed to leave Simeon, and they thought:

"If we're in trouble now, it's because we did wrong in the past with our brother Joseph."

When they arrived back in Canaan at their father's house they told him all that had happened. Jacob said:

"No. Benjamin cannot go to Egypt. Already Joseph is dead and Simeon is in prison."

But all the same, when they ran out of food, Jacob said to his sons:

"Go back to Egypt and get some more food."

"But Pharaoh's chief minister won't let us in unless we take Benjamin," they said.

"All right," said Jacob, "but take presents for this Egyptian. Perhaps God will influence him to be kind to us."

When they arrived at Joseph's house, Joseph cried with joy to see Benjamin. He had Simeon set free at once. His brothers gave him their presents, and bowed down in front of him. Joseph asked how their father was, and gave them a great feast.

Then Joseph had his brothers' bags filled with food.
And he had his own silver cup put secretly in
Benjamin's bag. The next day the eleven sons of Jacob
set off with their donkeys. Joseph sent his assistant
after them to catch them:

"You've stolen my master's cup!" he said.

"Never!" they said, "search our bags yourself. And if
any of us has taken it he should die!"

"Agreed! I will keep the thief as a slave."

He found the cup in Benjamin's bag. He took
Benjamin with him, but the brothers followed them to
Joseph's house, and threw themselves at his feet, and
begged him:

"God is punishing us for what we once did to our
brother Joseph. We will be your slaves."

Joseph replied: "Only the one who stole shall be my
slave."

Then Judah spoke:

"Excuse me, sir," he said, "but you asked us if our
father was still alive, and you wanted us to bring our
youngest brother. Our father did not want him to
come, because he loved him so much he could not
bear to part with him. If we don't bring him back it
will kill him. Take me please as a slave in his place."

From the Book of Genesis,
chapters 41 to 44.

The family is together again

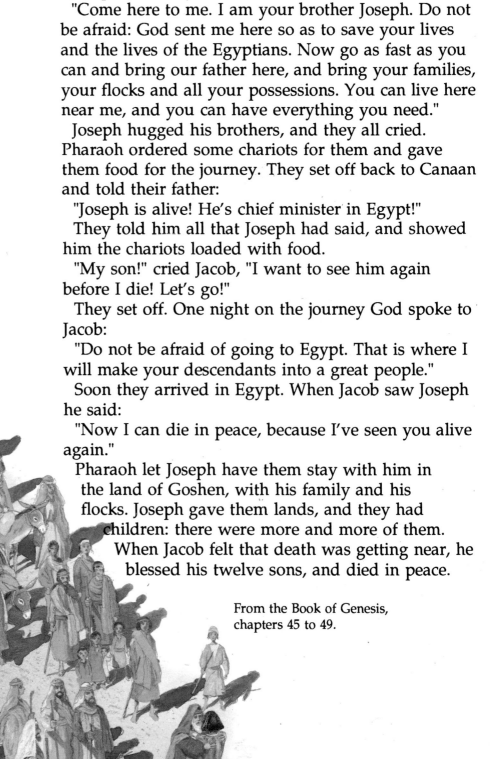

Why is Joseph so important in the Bible?

Because Joseph is an example of a person close to God. Joseph never became obsessed by power, sex, the desire for revenge, or violence. He was good, and he forgave those who had done him harm.

Joseph was very moved; he burst into tears and said:

"Come here to me. I am your brother Joseph. Do not be afraid: God sent me here so as to save your lives and the lives of the Egyptians. Now go as fast as you can and bring our father here, and bring your families, your flocks and all your possessions. You can live here near me, and you can have everything you need."

Joseph hugged his brothers, and they all cried. Pharaoh ordered some chariots for them and gave them food for the journey. They set off back to Canaan and told their father:

"Joseph is alive! He's chief minister in Egypt!"

They told him all that Joseph had said, and showed him the chariots loaded with food.

"My son!" cried Jacob, "I want to see him again before I die! Let's go!"

They set off. One night on the journey God spoke to Jacob:

"Do not be afraid of going to Egypt. That is where I will make your descendants into a great people."

Soon they arrived in Egypt. When Jacob saw Joseph he said:

"Now I can die in peace, because I've seen you alive again."

Pharaoh let Joseph have them stay with him in the land of Goshen, with his family and his flocks. Joseph gave them lands, and they had children: there were more and more of them.

When Jacob felt that death was getting near, he blessed his twelve sons, and died in peace.

From the Book of Genesis, chapters 45 to 49.

Slaves in Egypt

Some years later, Joseph died. Much later, a new Pharaoh who had not known Joseph came to the throne. He said to the people:

"The Israelites are beginning to outnumber us, and they are becoming more powerful than we are. Let's stop these people getting so strong, and make them our slaves."

He gave the Israelites harsh and exhausting work to do: they had to build two cities for Pharaoh. But the more harshly they were treated, the more they grew in numbers and the stronger they became. Pharaoh was very angry and he commanded:

"Throw all the new-born Hebrew boys into the Nile." ("Hebrew" was what the Egyptians called the Israelites).

Why are the descendants of Jacob called Israelites, or "children of Israel"?

Because Jacob's other name was "Israel"; so his children and grandchildren are called "children of Israel". Later they were also called the Jews.

From the Book of Exodus,
chapter 1, verses 8 to 22.

A baby saved from the water

What do other histories tell about Moses' story?

We do not know all the details. All we know is that Pharaoh Ramses II built his capital Raamses (nowadays called Qantir) using as slaves the foreigners whom the Egyptians called "Hebrews". The Bible writers started the story of Moses from his birth because they wanted to show the importance of this person who was chosen by God.

One day an Israelite woman had a baby boy. She managed to hide him for three months. Then, to save him from death, she put him in a basket of rushes on the edge of the Nile. The baby's sister hid near by to see what would happen to him. As usual, Pharaoh's daughter came down to bathe. She saw the basket, opened it and found the howling baby. She was sorry for him:

"It's a little Hebrew. Isn't he beautiful!" she said.

The baby's sister came out then and said:

"Would you like me to see if I can find a nurse to feed him among the Hebrew women?"

"Yes, you do that," said the Egyptian princess.

The baby's sister went off, and came back with the baby's mother, and the princess said to her:

"Take this baby and look after him, and I will pay you."

The mother took her baby and looked after him. When he was big she took him back to the princess. The princess brought him up as her own son, and named him Moses, which means "saved from the waters".

From the Book of Exodus, chapter 2, verses 1-10.

The burning bush

When Moses grew up he realized how harshly his people were being treated. One day he killed an Egyptian who was beating an Israelite. Pharaoh heard about it and ordered that Moses should be arrested and killed. But Moses escaped to the land of Midian. While he was there he got married and worked as a shepherd.

One day when he was guarding his flock at the foot of Mount Horeb, the mountain of God, he heard God calling to him from a burning bush. The bush seemed to be burning but did not turn to ashes. God said:

"Moses! I have seen the misery of my people in Egypt, and I know their sufferings. I want to set them free and bring them back to Canaan. Go to Pharaoh!"

Moses replied:

"But when I go to the Israelites and say to them that God has sent me to set you free, they will ask your name!"

"Tell them that God who has sent you to them says he is I AM."

From the Book of Exodus, chapter 2, verses 11 to 15, and chapter 3, verses 1 to 14.

Why did God say his name was I AM?

This mysterious name tells us that one name is not enough to tell us who God is. God is the one whom the Israelites were discovering through what happened to them, which they understood as "acts of God". The Israelites also had a Hebrew name for God, "Yahweh", but out of awe they never said it aloud. Often it is replaced by "the Lord".

Panic in Egypt

What is the point of all these disasters?

The story of "the ten plagues of Egypt" was told to show that God was fighting Pharaoh to liberate God's people. In this story the gods of the Egyptians were made to look ridiculous: the god Nile was hit by Moses with a stick, the animals whom the Egyptians worshipped as gods brought harm to the Egyptians, and the Egyptian sun-god was overcome when darkness covered the land!

Moses and his brother Aaron went to Pharaoh and said:

"Thus says the Lord, the God of Israel. 'Let my people go and pray to me in the desert'."

Pharaoh refused. Then God said to Moses:

"Let Aaron hit the Nile with his stick: it will turn to blood!"

Aaron did this, and the Nile water turned red with blood. The fish died and the river smelled terrible. But the Egyptian sorcerers could do this too. So Pharaoh still took no notice of Moses.

Then with his stick Aaron covered all of Egypt with billions of frogs. But still the Egyptian sorcerers could do the same. Pharaoh said to Moses:

"Get rid of these frogs and I will let your people go."

Moses agreed, and the frogs disappeared. Pharaoh was pleased about this, but he broke his promise and would not let them go.

Then God covered Egypt with a cloud of mosquitoes which attacked humans and animals. This time the sorcerers could not compete. They said to Pharaoh:

"It is the hand of God!"

But the Pharaoh did not want to know.

Then there came a plague of flies: they went all over the land, and all the animals began to die, except the animals belonging to the Israelites. Huge bites which turned into open wounds afflicted the Egyptians. But Pharaoh did not change his mind. Storms and hail crushed all of Egypt, except for the land

of Goshen where the Israelites lived. Pharaoh promised they could go if all this stopped. But again he broke his promise. God said to Moses:

"Warn Pharaoh that locusts are going to invade his country!"

Moses warned him, and the king's advisers begged him:

"Let these people go. Our country is being destroyed!"

But Pharaoh was angry and would not listen to Moses and Aaron. Great clouds of locusts devoured all the plants that were left and invaded the houses. But Pharaoh would not let the Israelites go.

Darkness then covered the whole land. Only the Israelites had light. Pharaoh said to Moses:

"Go! Go and pray to your God in the desert! You can take your wives and children, but leave your flocks behind!"

"We shall not leave one animal behind," said Moses.

Pharaoh changed his mind and would not let them go; he shouted:

"Leave my palace! And don't come back or I will kill you!"

"Right," said Moses, "I won't come back!"

From the Book of Exodus, chapters 7 to 10.

The great escape

God said to Moses:

"The time has come for me to show my power: to show that I am the Lord God. Let each family prepare a lamb. You shall sacrifice it at sunset. With its blood you shall mark the doorposts of your houses, then you shall roast the lamb. Eat it hastily, with unleavened bread, with your sandals on your feet, and your sticks in your hands, ready to go. This is the Passover of the Lord."

Moses told the people everything God had said. That night the eldest sons of all the Egyptians died as well as the first born of all their animals. The houses with the blood of the lamb marking the doorposts were passed over and did not suffer.

The Israelites escaped into the desert with their flocks and their possessions. Everything God had said had come to pass. In the future they would keep this day as the feast of the Passover, to remember what God had done.

From the Book of Exodus, chapter 12.

What is Passover?

Passover started as a feast when shepherds killed a lamb to celebrate the full moon of spring, probably the feast Moses asked Pharaoh to let the people go into the wilderness to celebrate. However, Passover became a very important festival, which helped the Israelites to remember the Exodus, and how God had delivered them from slavery in Egypt.

Crossing the sea

Where is this sea?

People believed for a long time that this was the Red Sea. In fact, the Israelites may have crossed the marshy land to the north, not far from Goshen. (See the map on page 31.)

Pharaoh was furious that they had gone, and he decided to chase the people of Israel with his chariots and his soldiers. The Israelites who were beside the sea were terrified when they saw them coming.

"Do not fear," said Moses. "The Lord will save us. This is the last you will see of the Egyptians!"

The Lord had told Moses what to do. The people should advance towards the sea. When Moses lifted his stick and stretched his arm over the sea, the sea would roll back and the people would be able to go through safely. God said:

"The Egyptians will chase you into the sea.

And then they will know that I am the Lord!"

Moses obeyed. The waters divided and the people of Israel, led by God, crossed without wetting their feet. The Egyptians chased after them right into the middle of the sea. The Lord said to Moses:

"Stretch out your hand again."

Moses did this, and the waters rushed back into their place: the whole Egyptian army was drowned. That day the people of Israel realized what God had done for them. They had faith in God, and in Moses God's servant.

From the Book of Exodus, chapter 14.

What does this story mean?

At the creation of the world, God separated the waters to make the earth appear. Now God is creating a nation by parting the waters so that they can pass from slavery to freedom, from death to life.

Hungry in the desert

What is manna?

Manna was the food God gave the Hebrew people to keep them alive in the desert wilderness. God may have led Moses to see that a sweet substance insects deposit, or the sap of bushes, could be used as food.

After travelling for six weeks the children of Israel reached the Sinai desert. They complained to Moses:

"You brought us here to die of hunger. In Egypt at least we had something to eat."

Then God said to Moses:

"I have heard their complaints. God and tell them that after sunset they will have meat, and tomorrow morning they will have plenty of bread. Then they will know that I am the Lord their God."

That very evening a flock of quails landed in the camp and the next morning the ground of the desert was covered with a thin crust. The people shouted:

"What is it?" For they did not know what it was.

Moses replied:

"It's the bread which God has given you."

From the Book of Exodus, chapter 16, verses 1 to 15

The ten commandments

The children of Israel continued their journey and camped in the Sinai desert. One day there was a terrible thunderstorm and a sound like a trumpet call high up in the mountain. The people shook with fear. The Lord was in the storm of fire. He called Moses to come up to him and said:

"I am the Lord your God, who brought you out of Egypt. These are my commandments:
You shall have no other gods but me.
You shall not make any image or statue to worship.
You shall not use the name of God to do evil.
You shall make the seventh day of each week a holy
  day of prayer and rest.
Respect your father and your mother.
You shall not kill.
You shall not steal.
You shall not commit adultery.
You shall not falsely accuse anyone.
You shall not try to get for yourself anything that
  belongs to someone else.
Here are my commandments written on blocks of stone. Keeping my commandments is your part of the agreement and covenant with me."

Moses spent forty days and nights on the mountain. When he came down his face was shining with joy.

From the Book of Exodus,
chapters 19, 20 and 21.

Why did God give the commandments?

God gave the commandments to help the people he had saved to live at peace with him and with each other. Later on Jesus summed up the commandments in these words: "You shall love the Lord your God, and your neighbour as yourself."

The golden calf

Still Moses did not return. The Israelites wanted a god they could see. So they gave Aaron, Moses' brother, all their gold earrings; Aaron melted them down and shaped the gold into a calf. When they saw the golden calf the Israelites cried out:

"This is the god who brought us out of Egypt!"

Aaron set up an altar for this god, and held a feast to worship it. The next day,

the people offered sacrifices, held a feast and began to sing and dance.

At that moment Moses came down the mountain with the two tablets of stone. When he saw the golden calf, he was furious. He threw down and broke the stone tablets and then burnt the golden calf and crushed it to bits. Then he said to the people:

"You have committed a terrible sin! But I will go back and beg the Lord to forgive you."

Moses went back to the Lord, and begged forgiveness. God told him to continue the journey, but God would not be with the Israelites in the same way as in the past.

From the Book of Exodus,
chapter 32, verses 1 to 34.

Why was it wrong to make a golden calf?

By worshipping the golden calf, the Israelites were being unfaithful to God. They were making a statue which was like the idols of the other peoples around them, in this case a fertility god in the form of a young bull.

The ark of the covenant

Do those stone tablets still exist?

No. They were lost during the destruction of the temple of Jerusalem by Nebuchadnezzar (see page 68).

What is the cloud of God's presence?

It was a cloud of smoke, like the smoke of incense which is burnt in some churches and temples. It symbolized the presence of God.

During the journey through the desert Moses wanted some sign that God had really chosen him and his people. One day he said to God:

"Let me see your face!"

God replied:

"I will go past you and say my name, because I want to show my love for you. But you will not see my face, because a human being cannot see it and stay alive. Hide in the crack in this rock, and when I pass I will shelter you with my hand. When I take my hand away you will see my back, as I go away."

Moses crossed Mount Sinai and the Lord went past him, as he had said. Then he made him write the commandments again on tablets of stone, and renewed his promise and covenant. Moses went back to the people, with his face shining with joy from his meeting with God. He had a special tent made in which he could keep the tablets of stone in their special box, called "the Ark of the Covenant".

The presence of God filled the tent and the cloud of God's presence was over the tent: at night a fire glowed in this cloud. When the cloud lifted, the people set out on the journey. If the cloud did not lift, they stayed in the same camp. God's presence went with the people all through the journey.

From the Book of Exodus, chapter 33, verses 18 to 23, and chapter 40, verses 16 to 38.

The death of Moses

The journey through the desert lasted forty years. When Moses was very old, he chose Joshua to be his successor.

Some time later, the Israelites arrived in the plain of Moab. Moses climbed Mount Nebo. From the mountain top God let him see the whole of the land of Canaan, and said to him:

"This land which you see is the land I promised to the descendants of your ancestors Abraham, Isaac and Jacob. I am showing it to you, but you will not live to enter it."

In fact Moses died in the plain of Moab as God had told him he would. He was buried in the valley and the Israelites mourned him for thirty days.

There was never to be another prophet in Israel like Moses: the Lord spoke with him face to face as a person speaks with a friend. God had sent him to work wonders in Egypt before Pharaoh and all the country. And with Israel Moses had authority, as the servant of God.

From the Book
of Deuteronomy,
chapter 34.

Did the journey across the desert really last forty years?

The number 40 is often used in the Bible for times of testing and meeting with God. Here the crossing of the desert is a picture which symbolises the whole history of Israel. It is also the story of each believer's journey through life: a long journey full of difficulties, of faith and doubt, temptations, longing for reassurance, discouragements and great joys.

Why was Moses so important?

Because God called him to be the liberator of the people of Israel, and to be the messenger of God to the people. He was the greatest prophet of Israel.

The promised land at last!

As they continued their journey, the Israelites arrived at a river called the Jordan. The Lord said to Joshua:
"Today the people of Israel will know that I am with you, just as I was with Moses."
Joshua told the people what the Lord had said. They set off to cross the deep river. The priests went in front carrying the ark of the covenant. When they

touched the water, the river stopped as if it was held back by a wall, while on the other side it flowed on to the sea. The priests let all the people cross on dry land before they went across themselves.

When they were all on the other side, near the town of Jericho, the river began to flow again.

From the Book of Joshua,
chapter 3, verses 7 to 17.

Did the river really stop flowing?

It is possible, because sometimes the banks of the Jordan collapse into the river and stop it flowing.

The siege of Jericho

What have archaeologists discovered about Jericho?

Archaeologists have found evidence that people lived in Jericho as long as 10,000 years ago. They have also found ruins of walls that were torn down about 300 years before Joshua is thought to have come to Jericho.

When the people of Israel reached Jericho they found the city gates shut. No one could go in or out. The Lord said to Joshua:

"I will give you Jericho, its king and its people. Each day for six days make a procession around the outside of the city: you, your soldiers, seven priests each carrying a ram's horn, and the ark of the covenant. On the seventh day, make the procession seven times around the city and tell the priests to sound their

rams' horns. The people must give a great shout and the walls will come tumbling down. This is how you will get into Jericho."

Joshua told the people what the Lord had said. They followed God's orders to the letter; and in this way on the seventh day the Lord handed over the city to them.

From the Book of Joshua,
chapter 6, verses 1 to 20.

The choice of God

Some time later Joshua called together at Shechem all the Israelites, who were divided into twelve tribes: each tribe had the name of one of Jacob's sons. He reminded them of all that the Lord had done for the people, from the time of Abraham up to their entry into the land of Canaan. Joshua went on:

"Choose this day whom you will serve, whether the gods of the peoples here in Canaan, or the Lord. As for me and my household, we will serve the Lord."

The people replied:

"We too will serve the Lord, for he is our God."

That day Joshua made a covenant for the people. He chose a huge rock and set it on end to remind them of their promise.

Later Joshua died at the age of a hundred and ten.

From the Book of Joshua,
chapter 24, verses 1 to 29.

The exploits of Samson

The Israelites settled all over the land of Canaan. Before long they were again doing what was wrong in God's eyes. So God left them to the mercy of the Philistines, a sea people.

There was an Israelite couple who could not have children. One day the angel of the Lord appeared to the wife and told her:

"You will give birth to a boy, who will be consecrated to God. To show that he will serve God, his hair must never be cut. He will begin to free Israel from the Philistines."

And so it turned out. She had a boy and called him Samson. He grew up, blessed by the Lord, to be very strong. One day he killed a lion with his bare hands. Another day he burnt the Philistines' fields by tying burning torches to the tails of a hundred foxes. Another time he fought and killed a thousand enemies, and his only weapon was the jawbone of a donkey.

But Samson fell in love with a Philistine woman, Delilah. And the Philistine leaders saw this as an opportunity to get rid of Samson. They came to see her and said:

"Use your charm to find out where Samson's strength comes from, and how to counteract it. We will pay you well!"

Delilah tried to discover Samson's secret, but he would not tell her. She went on and on asking him, and one day he gave in and told her:

"My hair has never been cut because I am consecrated to God. That is where my great strength comes from."

Delilah waited till Samson was asleep, called the Philistines and told them to cut off Samson's hair. When Samson woke up his strength was gone.

What is an angel?

An angel is a messenger from God, a visible sign of God's presence. Sometimes angels are described as having wings, to show that they belong to a higher world.

When he awoke, the Philistines put out his eyes and threw him in prison. Gradually his hair grew again, and Samson was sorry for his mistake.

The Philistines decided to organize a feast to celebrate their victory over Samson. They tied Samson between two pillars in the temple of their god, to mock him. But Samson prayed to the Lord:

"Lord, remember me. Give me strength for the last time, to fight back."

With all his force he pushed the two pillars, shouting:

"Let me die with the Philistines!"

The temple collapsed on top of him, and on top of the Philistines and their kings.

From the Book of Judges,
chapters 13 and 16.

Samuel, the child God called

Hannah, an Israelite woman, had no child, so she went to the temple at Shiloh and prayed that God would give her a child.

Soon she had a baby boy and called him Samuel. As soon as he was big enough she took him to the temple to help Eli the priest serve God. The years passed. At that time, people did not often hear God speaking to them; it seemed as if God had forgotten them. One night, when Eli was asleep in his room, Samuel heard God calling him, twice, as he lay near the Ark of the Covenant in the temple. Samuel did not know that it was God as he had never heard a call from God before. He thought it was Eli calling him, and he ran to Eli. Eli said:

"I didn't call you. Go back to bed."

This happened twice. The third time, Eli realized that it was the Lord who was calling the child. He told Samuel:

"Go back to bed. If it happens again, say: 'Speak, Lord, for your servant is listening.'"

Samuel went back to bed and God called him again:

"Samuel! Samuel!"

"Speak, for your servant is listening," replied Samuel.

God spoke to him in the temple.

Samuel grew up, and the people of Israel realized that he was a prophet of the Lord.

From the First Book of Samuel, chapter 3.

What did the priests do in the temples?

The priests led the prayers. They told the people of Israel about their history, reminded them about the laws and the covenant with God. They burned incense and offered sacrifices to God in the name of the faithful: they offered harvest produce or animals as sacrifices, most often lambs.

Saul, the first king of Israel

Why was oil used to consecrate a king?

In ancient times oil was used as a way to make the skin beautiful and special. In the consecration of a person, holy oil is the sign that God's spirit is making the future king special.

The Israelites wanted a king, like the other nations around them. Samuel said to them:

"I warn you, if you have a king, he will take your sons to be in his army and to work on his land, and your daughters to wait on him, and he will take part of your money in taxes. You will become his slaves and you will complain bitterly! God is your real king, why do you want another?"

But the people did not listen. So in the end God said to Samuel:

"Let them have what they want. Give them a king!"

God told Samuel whom he had chosen as king: it was Saul, who was well-known for his many gifts. Samuel poured the holy oil on Saul's head and said:

"The Lord God has chosen you as king. You shall be the leader of your people."

Saul led the people in war against all their enemies, but he was not faithful to God. In the end Samuel told him:

"God has sent me to tell you that you are no longer the king. Because you have rejected God's word, you will also be rejected, and God will find another king, better than you."

From the First Book of Samuel, chapters 8, 9, 10 and 15.

David, the shepherd who became king

The Lord said to Samuel:

"Take some holy oil and go to Bethlehem, to the house of Jesse. Invite him with his family to a sacrifice, and then you can secretly anoint as king the person I shall show you."

Samuel obeyed the Lord. When he arrived in Bethlehem he invited Jesse and his sons. When Samuel saw Eliab, the eldest, he thought:

"This must be the one God has chosen!"

"No, it's not this one," said the Lord. "God does not think the way humans do; humans look at people's appearance, but God sees their hearts."

One by one Jesse introduced six more sons. Samuel then asked if he had any other sons.

"Yes," said Jesse," there is David, the youngest, out watching the flocks."

"Send for him," said Samuel.

When David arrived, the Lord said to Samuel:

"This is the one! Anoint him king with the holy oil."

From that day onward the Spirit of the Lord was always with David.

Samuel returned home.

From the First Book of Samuel,
chapter 16, verses 1 to 13.

Why was David anointed in secret?

Because Saul would still be king for many years. David's anointing was a promise that he would officially be king in the future.

David fights the giant

Why did David win, when he was smaller than Goliath?

David explained this when he said that Goliath fought with weapons, but David fought with the help of God. And God had chosen him as the future king of Israel. Later on Jesus said that God had chosen the little people to be stronger than the powerful people.

David went to work for king Saul. The Philistines were again fighting the Israelites, and the two armies were facing each other. Goliath, a giant from the Philistine army, challenged the army of Israel for forty days: he demanded that one of the Israelite warriors should come and fight him in single combat. David said to king Saul:

"I am going to fight with him!"

"But you're only a boy!" replied Saul. "He's a real soldier and a giant!"

"The Lord will save me," said David.

"Go then," said Saul, "and God be with you."

David put five small stones in his shepherd's bag, and then he walked up to Goliath with a sling in his hand. Goliath looked at him with scorn:

"Come here and I'll feed you to the birds!" said he.

"I will fight you in the name of the Lord," said David. "God will hand you over to me, you and your army. And the whole land will know that Israel has a powerful God."

With his sling, David shot a stone, and hit Goliath in

the forehead. The giant
fell. Then David took
his sword and cut off
Goliath's head. When the
Philistines saw their
champion was dead, they
ran away.

From the First Book of Samuel,
chapter 17, verses 1 to 51.

Saul hunts for David

Saul was jealous of David's success. He was afraid that David might become king in his place, and he wanted to kill him. David and his friends had to escape and hide in the mountains.

Saul went to search for him with three thousand men. One day he went into a cave to relieve himself. As it happened this was the very cave where David and his friends were hiding. They whispered to David:

"The Lord told you that he would hand over your enemy to you and you would be able to do what you wanted with him. Now's your chance!"

David crept up behind Saul and cut off the corner of his coat, and then he whispered to his friends:

"I shall not kill the person God chose as our king."

Saul went out of the cave, and then David shouted:

"My Lord the king!"

Saul turned round and David bowed down before him, and said:

"I could have killed you there in the cave, but I did not, because I respect the fact that you were anointed king with the holy oil. All I did was cut off a corner of your coat. I am not bitter because you tried to kill me. God is our judge and God will avenge me, not I."

Saul began to weep:

"David, you are just, and I have done wrong. The Lord delivered me into your power and you did not kill me. May God reward you. Now I know that you will be king of Israel."

From the First Book of Samuel, chapter 24, verses 3 to 21.

What else is known about David?

The Bible tells us that David was a musician. He played the harp and composed songs for the worship of God. It is said that many of the Psalms were composed by him. Even today, Jews and Christians use these psalms for worship.

David takes over Jerusalem

Why did David choose Jerusalem as his capital?

Because this city, which belonged to the Canaanites, was the centre of Israel, and was situated on a hill, which made it easier to defend in case of attack.

Later on, Saul was killed in a battle with the Philistines. And seven years later, all the tribes of Israel recognized David as their king, and anointed him.

David decided to take over Jerusalem and make it his capital city. He and his men marched on the city. The people of Jerusalem would not let them in, but God was on their side, and he was able to win control of the city. With great joy the Israelites brought the ark of the covenant to the city, and from that time onwards Jerusalem was known as the "City of David". King David offered a sacrifice and threw off his royal clothes and danced to the Lord. As the people cheered the ark was set up in a special tent. David made other sacrifices to God, and blessed the people and gave out fruit and cakes to everyone.

From the Second Book of Samuel, chapter 5, verses 1 to 9, and chapter 6, verses 17 to 19.

A new promise
from God

65

David lived in a palace. One day he said to Nathan, the prophet:

"I live in a palace, but the Ark of God only has a tent!"

"You must do what you feel is right," said Nathan.

But the Lord said to Nathan:

"Tell David: 'I have no need of a house, and I have never had one. But I will give you a house, that is a royal house: your son will rule over the people of Israel. And he is the one who will build me a house. I shall be a father to him, and he will be a son to me. If he does wrong I will correct him, but I will never cease to love him.'"

Nathan duly reported the Lord's words to David.

From the Second Book of Samuel,
chapter 7, verses 1 to 17.

What kind of house was God speaking of?

In the past "house" could mean the building, or the family who lived in it. Here, God is speaking of Solomon, David's future son.

King Solomon and the stolen baby

David reigned for many years and made his country larger. When he died his son Solomon became king. He was famous for his great wisdom.

One day two women came to ask him about a problem:

"I beg you, my Lord," said one, "listen to me. We two women live by ourselves in a big house, and we each had a son. Her baby died during the night, and while I was asleep she took my baby and she claims he is hers, and she won't give him back."

"That's not true," said the other. "My baby is the one who is alive and yours is dead!"

Solomon said:

"Bring me a sword, cut the baby in half and give half to each mother."

Immediately one of the women cried out:

"My Lord, give her the baby, but please, please don't kill him!"

"Cut him in half," said the other woman. "Then he won't belong to anybody."

Then Solomon gave another order:

"Give the baby to the first woman; she is his mother."

All the people heard about this judgment and believed that Solomon had God's wisdom.

From the First Book of Kings, chapter 3, verses 16 to 28.

The most beautiful temple in the world

Solomon sent a message to his friend Hiram, king of Tyre, in Lebanon:

"I have decided to build a house for the Lord in Jerusalem, according to his words to my father David. So please order the cedars of Lebanon to be cut down for the building. I will send workers to work on this with yours, and I will pay them all what you think is right."

Hiram was very pleased at this and said:

"Praise the Lord for giving David such a wise son to rule this great people!"

He sent Solomon cedar wood and cypress. In return he received corn and olive oil. Solomon sent 30,000 men to work in Lebanon. For seven years, 10,000 stone carriers and 80,000 stone cutters worked to build the temple, under the direction of 3,300 architects. The whole interior was covered with gold leaf. The temple was immense and magnificent to give glory to God.

From the First Book of Kings, chapter 5, verses 16 to 32, and chapter 6.

What was the temple like?

The temple was in the centre of a large, sacred area. It had three rooms: the Entrance, the Holy Place where only the priests were allowed to enter, and the "Holy of Holies" where the Ark of the Covenant was kept. Only the High Priest entered it, and only once a year. The altar, where animals were sacrificed, was in front of the temple.

Jerusalem on fire

What happened to the people who were deported?

In Babylon they were exiles, but they were not in prison. They could build houses and make gardens and follow their religion, but they also had to work for the Babylonians on construction sites and in the fields. Some of them did so well in Babylon that they never returned to Jerusalem.

After David and Solomon, there were other kings in Jerusalem. But often they did things that were wrong in God's eyes: they made alliances and got involved in wars with neighbouring countries.

In the reign of Jehoiachim, who became king at the age of eighteen, Nebuchadnezzar, the king of Babylon, attacked Jerusalem because it was allied with Egypt. Jehoiachim and his court surrendered.

Nebuchadnezzar carried away the treasures of the temple and the palace, and broke the beautiful things Solomon had made. He took Jehoiachim to Babylon as his prisoner, with Jehoiachim's wives, government ministers, seven thousand soldiers, a thousand craftsmen, and all who were of the right age for fighting. He left no one behind except the weakest and poorest, and put Zedekiah in charge of them as king; he was Jehoiachim's uncle.

Zedekiah soon betrayed Nebuchadnezzar by making an alliance with Egypt. So Nebuchadnezzar returned to attack Jerusalem. He sent for Zedekiah, killed his sons in front of him and then put out his eyes and took him in chains to Babylon. He deported the rest of the population and left no one behind except a few farm workers and wine growers. Some years later he had Jerusalem burned to the ground.

From the Second Book of Kings, chapter 24, verses 8 to 17, and chapter 25, verses 1 to 12.

Freed from exile!

Fifty years later, Cyrus, king of Persia, conquered Babylon and became the master of the Near East. He was inspired by God to make this announcement:

"The Lord God has given me all the kingdoms of the world. And God has told me to rebuild the temple in Jerusalem. Will all those who belong to God's people return there and rebuild the temple of the God of Israel. And will all the people living there help in every way."

So 150,000 Israelites set off for Jerusalem from Babylon. It took them at least fifteen years to rebuild the temple. On the day of the Passover they held a great feast to celebrate its completion.

From the Book of Ezra, chapters 1 to 6.

Why did Cyrus free the Israelites?

Cyrus freed all the peoples who had been deported by the Babylonians. He thought that it was wise government to allow the peoples of his empire some freedom. In this way his empire was peaceful, even in the most distant provinces.

Judith, the courageous widow

Long after their exile in Babylon and their return to Jerusalem, the Jews loved to tell this story:

Nebuchadnezzar was an ambitious king; he told his general Holophernes to conquer all the Near East. One day Holophernes' army arrived at the gates of the Jewish town of Bethulia, and gained control of the water supply. Soon the townspeople were dying of thirst and begging their king Ozias to surrender the town. But he replied:

"Let us be brave. Let us hold out for another five days. God will not forsake us. But if God has not rescued us by then, we'll surrender."

Judith heard what the king had said. She was a young and beautiful widow who had faith in God. She said to the rulers of the city:

"It is better to ask God to help us, than to wait and see what God will do for us. God will hear us if we ask. Have faith in me."

When Judith was alone she prayed:

"God, you put down the mighty from their thrones, look at the pride of our enemies: they are defying you. God of the little people, the weak, those without hope, save your people through the efforts of a humble woman."

Then Judith put on her very best clothes and perfume and jewels. Off she went to the enemy camp and asked to see general Holophernes.

He was overcome by her beauty and asked her to dinner. When he was drunk Judith cut off his head and ran back with it to Bethulia. She showed it to the citizens and said:

"Here is the head of Holophernes. God has conquered him by the strength of a woman!"

The people hung the head on the ramparts of the town, and went off to invade the enemy camp. When Holophernes' men saw them coming they ran to his tent to warn him. But they found his headless body and they all panicked. This gave the Israelites the chance to loot the camp. The Israelites were delighted, sang Judith's praises and made a laurel crown for her. Judith said to them:

"Sing God's praises and call upon him. Down with all who attack God's people!"

From the Book of Judith,
chapters 7 to 16.

Why is this story included in the Bible?

The story of Judith shows how God is never on the side of the proud, or those who use their power to crush others. God is on the side of the little people and the weak.
But it is not good enough to pray and wait for God to put things right. Judith gives us an example: her faith in God led to action.

Esther the brave

This is another story the Jews used to tell:

Xerxes, the king of Persia, held a great banquet for all the important people in his kingdom; the banquet lasted six months, and at the end of it he invited all the citizens to a feast, for seven days, in his palace in Suza.

On the last day the king was completely drunk, and wanted everyone to admire the beauty of his wife Vashti. But Vashti refused to come when he sent for her, and Xerxes became very angry indeed. He commanded that she should no longer be queen, and that beautiful young women should be brought to him so that he could choose someone to take her place.

One of these young women was Esther; she was an orphan and had been adopted by Mordecai, a Jew who worked at the palace. The king fell in love with Esther and married her without realizing she was Jewish. Haman, however, the king's chief minister, hated Mordecai and wanted to kill all the Jews. He had even decided on the day for the massacre. Mordecai discovered this plot and begged Esther to speak to the king about it.

Esther prayed to God. She would be put to death if she went to the King when he did not wish to see her. But she found the courage to invite the king to a banquet the next day, and the king accepted.

That same night, the king remembered that Mordecai had once saved his life. He wanted to reward him, and he asked Haman's advice. Haman thought it was himself the king wished to reward, so he suggested that the reward should be to ride in a procession wearing royal clothes. The king was delighted with this idea.

"Very well," he said, "prepare all this for Mordecai."

Haman went pale, because his plan was to kill Mordecai, not to honour him. That evening, at the banquet, Esther revealed to the king that she was Jewish, and that Haman was planning to massacre her people.

The king had Haman executed, and stopped the massacre. Mordecai had his reward: he rode in procession, wearing royal robes and a golden crown, and he took Haman's place as chief minister.

It was a great day of rejoicing for the Jews. Later they kept a festival in memory of how Esther had rescued them, and called it Purim (which means "lottery") because luck had turned against Haman, and those who wanted to kill all the Jews had been overcome.

From the Book of Esther.

Is the feast of Purim still kept today?

Yes. In memory of the story of Esther, Jews celebrate this feast once a year in February or March. It is a joyful feast when children wear fancy dress, as at a carnival.

Under foreign occupation

The Jews liked to tell stories of brave people who stood up for their God and their people in times of war and exile.

Their country was conquered and occupied by great empires: the Persian Empire, the Greek Empire and finally the Roman Empire; the Romans were in control of the country in the time of Jesus.

At the time of the Greek Empire, the Jews tried to rebel and break free from foreign occupation. The people pictured on this page preferred to die, rather than give up their faith in God.

One great leader at this time was Judas Maccabeus. He and his brothers stirred up the people to have courage and hope. They led their people in many battles. Judas won back Jerusalem and restored the temple of God there. When he had won his battles with the Greek Empire, he made a treaty with the Romans, to try to get support in keeping his country free in the future.

In the end he was killed in battle. All Israel made great lamentation for him, they mourned many days and said:

"How is the mighty fallen, who saved Israel!"

This is a song that was written about Judas:

He extended the glory of his people;
  like a giant he put on his breastplate.
He was like a lion in his deeds,
  like a lion's cub roaring for food,
He searched out and pursued those who broke
  the law.
Law-breakers shrank back for fear of him;
  all the evildoers were confounded;
  and deliverance prospered by his hand.
But he made Jacob glad by his deeds,
  and his memory is blessed for ever.
He was renowned to the ends of the earth;
  he gathered in those who were perishing.

From the Book of Maccabees.

The sufferings of Job

There was once an important man called Job. He was good, just and faithful. He had ten children, and many servants, and huge flocks of sheep.

One day Satan began to take an interest in him. Satan approached God.

"Where have you come from?" asked the Lord.

"I've been going to and fro and here and there," said the devil.

"I hope you have noticed Job," said the Lord, "there is no one better than Job."

Satan replied:

"That's because you protect him and help him. But I bet he would soon change his tune if things went badly for him!"

"Do what you want," said the Lord. "That will prove whether he is really good or not."

Satan decided to do just that. And before long, Job had lost everything he had: his cattle, donkeys, sheep, his wealth and his children. His body was covered with sores. So he tore his clothes and shaved his head as signs of mourning, threw himself down on the ground and said:

"I came into this world with nothing, and I will leave it with nothing. The Lord has given, and the Lord has taken away. Blessed be the name of the Lord!"

Because his skin disease was infectious, Job had to go and live on a trash heap outside the city. His wife told him to curse God for what had happened to him; his friends told him it must be all his own fault.

Job cried out to God:

"Why am I suffering so much when I have done nothing wrong? I've always helped the poor and people in trouble. I'm so miserable I want to die!"

The Lord answered him:

"Did you create the world? Have you any idea how huge the universe is? How can you expect to understand everything that happens?"

Job answered:

"I spoke without thinking, and said stupid things. But now I trust in you."

So the devil was proved wrong. And before long Job recovered his health and his children, and was twice as rich as before.

From the Book of Job.

Why did God let Job suffer so much?

This story does make God sound cruel. But it tells us that suffering is not a punishment from God for those who behave badly. But the suffering of an innocent person like Job is still impossible to understand. By the passion of his son Jesus, God shares in human suffering even to the point of death. Jesus' resurrection showed that death did not have the last word.

God is like a potter

What is a prophet?

A prophet is a person whose life and words are inspired by God. A prophet tells human beings what God requires of them as history unfolds. The greatest prophets were Isaiah, Jeremiah and Ezekiel.

One day the Lord spoke to the prophet Jeremiah:

"Go to the potter's workshop, and there you will hear my message."

Jeremiah went off to the potter's workshop, and watched the potter as he tried to make a clay pot which kept going wrong. So the potter reworked the clay in a new way, and made a beautiful vase.

Then Jeremiah understood what the Lord was saying to him:

"Can I not do with Israel just what the potter has done with the clay? Just like the clay in the potter's hands, so is Israel in my hands."

Jeremiah realized that God was trying to shape the people of Israel into the chosen people of God.

From the Book of Jeremiah, chapter 18, verses 1 to 10.

The song of the three children in the fire

This is a story the Jews loved to tell at the time when Antiochus was persecuting them.

In Babylon, King Nebuchadnezzar set up a gold statue and commanded all the people to worship it. Three young Jews, Shadrach, Meshach and Abednego, refused. The king was very angry and said:

"Is it true that you refuse to worship my gods? If you do not worship them, I will have you thrown into a burning fiery furnace, and your God will never rescue you from that."

Shadrach, Meshach and Abednego said to the king:

"That is not our concern. If our God can rescue us he will. And even if he doesn't, there is no way we will worship your gods."

Nebuchadnezzar was furious, and he ordered them to be thrown into the burning furnace. Shadrach stood among the flames and prayed:

"Lord, do not abandon us in our hour of need." Then all three began to sing praises to God.

Nebuchadnezzar was watching them, and suddenly he saw four people in the burning fiery furnace. He was amazed, and said to his counsellors:

"Didn't we throw three young people into the furnace? I've just seen four, all alive, and the fourth looked like a god."

He let Shadrach, Meshach and Abednego out of the furnace, and they were not even singed by the flames. Then Nebuchadnezzar said:

"Blessed be the God who sent his angel to rescue them. They had faith in God, and disobeyed me, because they were faithful to God!"

From the Book of Daniel,
chapter 3, verses 14 to 28.

Who was the fourth person who appeared in the fire?

The fourth person was an angel of God. The story reminded the Jews when they were persecuted that God supports his people in trouble: God holds back the fire, and makes the flames as cool as the morning wind.

Daniel in the lions' den

The Jews also used to tell this story:

Daniel was an Israelite who was a friend of Darius, the king of Persia. But some of the courtiers were jealous of him. One day they saw him praying in his room. They went off and said to the king:

"Didn't you decree that anyone who prays to any god or anyone else but you, should be thrown to the lions?"

"Yes," said the king, "that is the law of Persia. That law can never be changed."

"Well," they said, "Daniel, one of the Israelite exiles, is disobeying you. He prays three times a day."

The king was distressed to hear this, and he racked his brains all day to find a way to save Daniel. But the courtiers would not let him forget his decree. So he finally ordered Daniel to be thrown to the lions. He said to Daniel:

"Your God, whom you serve so faithfully, will rescue you!"

Daniel was thrown into the lions' den, and a huge stone was put across the mouth of the den to prevent any escape. The king went back to his palace but he could not eat or sleep. Early next morning he rushed to the den. He called Daniel desperately:

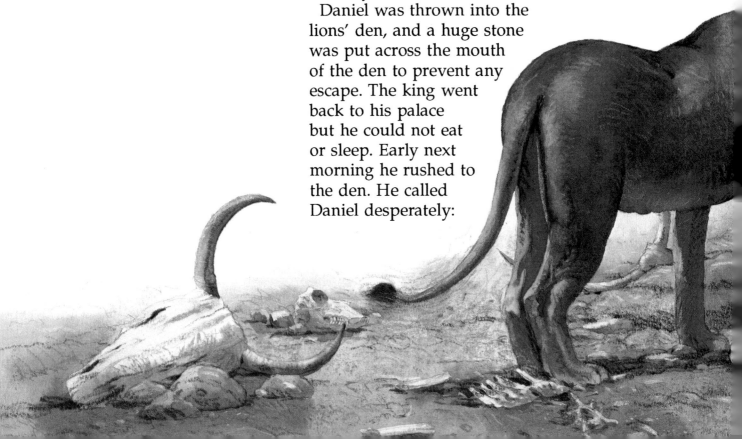

"Daniel, has your God, whom you serve so faithfully, been able to save you?"

"May the king live for ever," replied Daniel. "My God sent an angel to shut the lions' mouths. They did not attack me, because they knew I had done them no harm."

The king was overjoyed, and had Daniel brought out of the den. There was not a scratch on him. The king then sought out Daniel's accusers and threw them into the lions' den with their families. The lions ate them up immediately. Then King Darius wrote a message to all his subjects:

"Peace be with you! You must worship the God of Daniel, because he is the eternal and living God. He rescues and saves, and his kingdom will never end."

From the Book of Daniel, chapter 6, verses 12 to 28.

Jonah runs away from God

The Bible story-tellers were quite happy to make animals act as servants of God: here the sea, the wind, and the fish all make Jonah go to Nineveh. Later, Jesus spoke of Jonah's three days in the fish's stomach as a symbol of the three days Jesus would spend in the tomb before his resurrection.

One day a man called Jonah received a message from the Lord:

"Go to Nineveh, and tell the inhabitants that I have had enough of their wrongdoing!"

Jonah thought this would be dangerous; so he decided to get on a ship going in the opposite direction. But he could not escape so easily. A great storm arose, and all the passengers were praying to their gods, while Jonah was asleep.

"Get up!" the captain shouted at him. "You should be praying to your God to save us from the storm."

"There is someone on board who brings bad luck," said the sailors. "Let's draw lots to see who it is."

Jonah was the unlucky winner. The captain asked him:

"What can we do to you, to make the sea calm down?"

"Throw me in the sea," said Jonah, "because I am the cause of the trouble."

The sailors threw Jonah in the sea, and the storm stopped. But a great fish swallowed Jonah, and Jonah was in the fish's stomach for three days and three nights. He prayed:

"Out of the deep I call on you, O Lord. From the jaws of death hear my cry. Bring me back to life and I will praise your name."

So the Lord made the fish spew Jonah up on dry land.

Again the Lord spoke to Jonah:

"Go to Nineveh and take my message there."

So Jonah went to Nineveh and ran through the streets shouting:

"In forty days, Nineveh will be destroyed!"

84

Why was Jonah angry?

He felt foolish because he had announced destruction of the city and it did not happen. In fact he did not understand that God loves all people and not only the Jews; and that God forgives all who admit their faults.

At once the people of Nineveh gave up their wrong-doing and believed in God. They repented and fasted. Even the king did this and told the people:

"Pray to God as hard as you can, and do no evil. Perhaps God will change his mind."

God did change his mind, and Jonah was furious:

"Lord," he said, "I should have known that you were patient and full of love and slow to punish. What a fool you have made me look now. I'd rather die than put up with this."

Jonah built himself a hut near the city and went inside. During the night God made a tree grow to give him shade and cheer him up; Jonah was pleased with the tree. But the next day God sent a worm to attack the tree and it dried up, and a burning wind made Jonah feel ill; he begged for death. God replied:

"Are you so concerned just about a tree?"

"Yes, I'd rather die than go on like this."

"Listen," said God, "this tree grew up in one night and then died, and you are upset that I let the tree die. And yet you are angry that I am not destroying the city of Nineveh, in which there are more than a hundred and twenty people who do not know their right hand from their left."

From the Book of Jonah.

The one who will come

The words of the prophet Isaiah:
One day a descendant of David will be born.
On him the Spirit of the Lord will rest.
He will not judge by outward appearances
  or be led astray by what people tell him.
With justice he will judge the poor
  and defend the weak.
The wolf will live with the lamb
  and the cow and the bear will be friends.
No one will harm another person,
    for the earth will be filled with the love of God,
    as the waters cover the sea.

From the Book of Isaiah,
chapter 11, verses 1 to 9.

Who was Isaiah speaking about?

Isaiah lived eight hundred years before the birth of Jesus. He is speaking of a future king, descended from David, and sent by God. Over the centuries many Jews waited for the coming of this king, called the Messiah, who had come to show the path to peace, justice and love.

THE NEW TESTAMENT

The message to Mary

Why does the Bible tell us about these things that happened before Jesus was born?

This is the way the Gospels of Matthew and Luke show the double origin of Jesus: he was born to Mary and was truly human. But he was also "conceived by the Holy Spirit" which shows he was truly the Son of God.

About two thousand years ago a young woman called Mary lived in Nazareth, a village in Galilee. She was engaged to Joseph, who was descended from David. One day the angel Gabriel came from God to visit Mary, and said:

"Greetings, Mary, the Lord is with you."

Mary was astonished. The angel went on:

"Do not be afraid. You have found favour with God. You will bear a son, and you will name him Jesus. He will reign over the house of Jacob for ever, and his kingdom will never end."

Mary said to the angel:

"How can this be, since I am not married?"

"The Holy Spirit will come to you," said Gabriel, "and the power of the Most High will overshadow you. Your child will be called the Son of God."

Then Mary said:

"Here am I, the servant of the Lord. Let it be with me according to your word."

Then the angel departed from her.

From the Gospel of Luke, chapter 1, verses 26 to 38.

The amazing birth of Jesus

Some months later the Roman emperor Augustus ordered a census of all the inhabitants of his empire, which stretched all round the Mediterranean Sea. Each man had to register his family in the town where he had been born.

Joseph and Mary, who was pregnant, left Nazareth to go and register in Bethlehem, in the region of Judea. When they got there her baby was born, in the middle of the night. She wrapped him in bands of cloth and laid him in a manger in a stable, because there was no room for them in the inn.

In the fields near the town there were shepherds keeping watch over their sheep. Suddenly an angel of the Lord stood before them, and the glory of the Lord shone round about them. The angel said:

"Do not be afraid; I bring you good news of great joy for all the people. To you is born this day, in the city of David, the Messiah who has come to save you. You will find him there, lying in a manger."

What proof is there that Jesus existed?

Experts on the Gospels of Matthew, Mark, Luke and John have shown that the person they describe could not have been invented independently by all four. And Jesus is also mentioned by Jewish and Roman historians of that period.

Was Jesus really born on 25 December?

The exact date is not given in the Bible. Around the year 350 this date was chosen, by Christians in Rome. It was the date of the Roman pagan festival of the Unconquered Sun, when the winter days started to get longer again. For Christians the birth of Jesus was like the moment when the light grew stronger than the darkness.

And suddenly there was with the angel a multitude of the heavenly host, praising God, and saying:

"Glory to God in the highest, and peace to his people on earth!"

When the angels had left, the shepherds said to each other:

"Let's go to Bethlehem and see what the Lord has made known to us."

They hurried off and found Mary and Joseph and the baby in the manger. The shepherds told them what they had seen and heard and all were amazed. But Mary treasured all these words and pondered them in her heart.

From the Gospel of Luke,
chapter 2, verses 1 to 19.

The wise men and the star

In the time of King Herod, wise men from the east came to Jerusalem asking:

"Where is the child who has been born King of the Jews? We have seen his star in the east and have come to show respect to him."

Whe he heard a new King of the Jews had been born, King Herod was very worried. He asked the religious leaders where the Messiah would be born, and they replied:

"At Bethlehem, according to the prophet Micah."

Herod sent for the wise men and said to them:

"Go to Bethlehem and find the child, and tell me, so that I can go and pay my respects too."

The wise men set out, and there, ahead of them, went the star that they had seen in the east. It stopped over the place where the child was. They went in and saw the child with Mary, his mother. They bowed down and gave him their gifts, gold, frankincense and myrrh. Then they were warned by a dream not to return to Herod, so they returned to their country by another route.

From the Gospel of Matthew,
chapter 2, verses 1 to 12.

Who were the wise men?

The wise men were people who studied the stars. The first people we read about in Matthew's Gospel who came to worship Jesus are foreigners from the east. Later it was thought that there were three of them, because the Bible mentions three gifts, and they were even given names: Caspar, Melchior and Balthasar. They are even called kings!

Jesus is lost

What did Jesus mean by "in my Father's house"?

In this story he meant the temple, God's house. Jesus was twelve, a year younger than the age when young men were required to attend the Passover feast. Luke's gospel shows us that Jesus was really at home in the temple, because he was the Son of God.

Each year Jesus' parents went to Jerusalem for the Jewish festival of Passover. When Jesus was twelve years old, he went with them.

At the end of the festival, Mary and Joseph set off for home but did not notice that Jesus was not with their group. In the evening they realized that he was not with them. They went straight back to Jerusalem to look for him, and after three days they found him in the temple: Jesus was sitting among the religious teachers, listening to them and asking them questions. Those present were amazed at his understanding and his replies. Mary was astonished, and said to him:

"Child, why have you treated us like this? Your father and I have been so worried."

Jesus said:

"Why were you searching for me? Did you not know that I must be in my Father's house?"

But his parents did not understand.

Jesus went back to Nazareth with them, and was obedient to them. His mother treasured all these things in her heart. Jesus grew up in mind and body, and in friendship with others, and with God.

From the Gospel of Luke, chapter 2, verses 41 to 52.

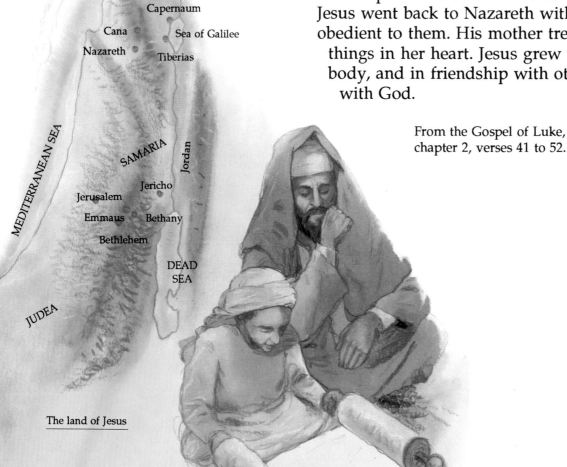

GALILEE
Capernaum
Cana
Nazareth
Sea of Galilee
Tiberias
MEDITERRANEAN SEA
SAMARIA
Jordan
Jericho
Jerusalem
Emmaus
Bethany
Bethlehem
DEAD SEA
JUDEA

The land of Jesus

The baptism of Jesus

Many years later, when Tiberius was Roman Emperor and Pontius Pilate was governor of Judea, John the Baptist appeared in the desert. From before John's birth, God had chosen him to be a prophet. He called people to return to God and change their lives. The people of Jerusalem and Judea were coming to be baptized by him in the Jordan, confessing their sins.

Jesus, who was nearly thirty, also came to be baptized. As he came out of the water he saw the Spirit of God coming down to him in the form of a dove, and a voice was heard from heaven, saying:

"You are my beloved Son; with you I am well pleased."

Then Jesus was driven by the Spirit to spend forty days in the desert.

From the Gospel of Mark,
chapter 1, verses 4 to 13.

Why did Jesus go into the desert after his baptism?

The desert was a place where people could get away from everyday life, and think about what was important in their lives. Jesus spent forty days there, and this reminds us that the people of Israel spent forty years in the desert after the exodus from Egypt. In this way Jesus prepared to preach the word of God.

Fishers of men and women

What is a disciple?

A disciple is a person who is learning from a teacher or leader, and wants to be like him or her. Jesus chose twelve of his disciples to be apostles: Simon Peter, James, John, Andrew, Philip, Bartholomew, Matthew, Thomas, another James, Thaddeus, Judas and Simon the Zealot.

After his time in the desert, when he was tempted to do his work for God not in God's way, but by making himself famous and powerful, Jesus returned to Galilee. One day, beside the Sea of Galilee, he saw two fishermen, Simon and his brother Andrew, casting a net into the sea. Jesus said:

"Come with me and I will make you fishers of men and women."

Simon and Andrew left their nets and followed him.

A little further on, Jesus saw James and John in a fishing boat with their father, Zebedee. They were mending their nets. Jesus called them. At once James and John left their father and went off to follow Jesus. These four people were Jesus' first disciples.

From the Gospel of Mark,
chapter 1, verses 16 to 20.

The wedding at Cana

One day there was a wedding in the village of Cana, and Mary, Jesus and his disciples were invited. At the wedding feast they ran out of wine. Mary said to Jesus:

"They haven't any more wine."

Jesus replied:

"My hour has not yet come."

But Mary believed that Jesus could do something, and she said to the servants:

"Do whatever he tells you."

Jesus told them:

"Fill the water jars with water and serve it."

They obeyed. The master of the feast tasted the water, which had been changed into wine. Not knowing where the wine came from, he said to the bridegroom:

"People usually serve the best wine first. But you have kept the best wine to the end!"

This was the first sign of who Jesus really was; and his disciples believed in him.

From the Gospel of John, chapter 2, verses 1 to 11.

A paralysed man is cured

A few days later, Jesus was in a house in Capernaum. People had heard he was there and a great crowd gathered. Jesus was speaking the word of God to them. Four men were trying to bring a paralysed man to him, but they could not get near him because of the crowd. So they climbed on the roof of the house, made a hole in the roof and lowered the man through the opening on his stretcher. When Jesus saw their faith, he said to the paralysed man:

"My son, your sins are forgiven."

The religious leaders who were there thought:

"He has no right to say that. Only God can forgive sins!"

Jesus knew what they were thinking, and said:

"Which is easier to say: 'Your sins are forgiven' or 'Get up and walk'? You must understand that I have the power to forgive sins."

Then he turned to the paralysed man, and said:

"Get up and go home!"

The man got up and went. Everyone was amazed, and gave thanks to God, saying:

"We have never seen anything like this!"

From the Gospel of Mark,
chapter 2, verses 1 to 12.

How could Jesus heal people?

We know that there were other healers at the time of Jesus. Jesus had the power to heal, but he did not use it to make himself famous. By healing people he was showing God's love for people and telling people about the Kingdom of God.

The secret of happiness

Yes. "Beatus" in Latin meant "happy". In these words Jesus is saying that the way to be happy is the opposite of what many people think, and Jesus is showing the way to be truly happy.

One day, when he saw a large crowd following him, Jesus climbed up the mountain. He sat down and said these amazing words:

"Happy are the poor in spirit, for theirs is the kingdom of heaven.

Happy are those who mourn, for they will be comforted.

Happy are the meek, for they will inherit the earth.

Happy are those who hunger and thirst for justice, for they will be filled.

Happy are the merciful, for they will receive mercy.

Happy are the pure in heart, for they will see God.

Happy are the peacemakers, for they will be called children of God.

Happy are those who are persecuted for the sake of justice, for theirs is the kingdom of heaven.

Happy are you, when people persecute you because you follow me.

Rejoice, because you will have a great reward in heaven."

From the Gospel of Matthew, chapter 5, verses 1 to 12.

Words of life

Jesus said to the crowd:

"When you pray, say: 'Our Father in heaven, hallowed be your name. Your kingdom come. Your will be done on earth as it is in heaven. Give us this day our daily bread. And forgive us our debts, as we also have forgiven our debtors. And do not bring us to the time of trial, but rescue us from the evil one.'"

Another time, a religious teacher wanted to test Jesus, and asked him:

"Master, which commandment in the law is the greatest?"

Jesus replied:

"'You shall love the Lord your God with all your heart, and with all your soul, and with all your mind.' This is the greatest and first commandment. And the second is like it: 'You shall love your neighbour as yourself'. All the law and the prophets are summed up in these two commandments."

From the Gospel of Matthew,
chapter 6, verses 9 to 13, and
chapter 22, verses 35 to 40.

The story of the sower

What is a parable?

A parable is a simple story, which is told to help people understand something difficult or important.

One day there was such a large crowd around Jesus, when he was teaching beside the lake, that he got into a boat to tell this parable:

"A sower went out to sow. Some seeds fell on the path, and the birds came and ate them up. Others fell on stony ground, where they did not have much soil. They sprang up quickly, but when the sun rose, they were scorched. Others fell among thorns and were choked. But other seeds fell on good soil and brought forth grain, some a hundredfold, some sixty, some thirty.

Let anyone with ears listen."

From the Gospel of Matthew, chapter 13, verses 1 to 9.

The treasure and the pearl

Jesus also told these parables:
"The kingdom of God is like a treasure hidden in a field. A man finds the treasure and is delighted. He hides the treasure again, goes and sells all he has and comes back to buy the field.

The kingdom of God is also like a beautiful pearl. A merchant has been hunting for beautiful pearls and in the end he finds this one. He will happily sell all he has to buy the beautiful pearl."

From the Gospel of Matthew,
chapter 13, verses 44 to 46.

The rich young man

What is eternal life?

Eternal life is life with God. Life can be lived with God at any time, but after death it is lived to the full.

A young man came to Jesus and asked:
"Master, what must I do to have eternal life?"
"Why are you asking me?" said Jesus. "Keep the commandments of our religion."
"Which ones?" he asked.
"Do not kill, do not steal, do not lie, respect your father and mother, do not take another person's wife or husband, love your neighbour as yourself."
"I have obeyed all these laws," said the young man. "What else must I do?"
"If you want to be perfect," said Jesus, "go and sell all you have and give the money to the poor. Then you will be rich in God's eyes. Then come and follow me."
When the young man heard these words, he went away sadly, because he was very rich.

From the Gospel of Matthew,
chapter 19, verses 16 to 22.

Living water

Jesus was travelling across the region of Samaria with his disciples. One day, about noon, Jesus was sitting on his own beside a well, which is called "Jacob's well", when a woman came from the town of Sychar to draw water.

"Give me some water to drink," Jesus asked her.

"What!" she said, "you are a Jew, and you ask me, a Samaritan, to give you water to drink!" (The Jews hated the Samaritans, because the Samaritans claimed that God should be worshipped on Mount Gerizim in Samaria, and not in Jerusalem.)

"If you knew what God can give," said Jesus, "and if you knew who I am, then you would be asking me for water, and not the other way round."

"You have nothing to put the water in," said the woman, "and the well is deep. So how could you give me water?"

Jesus said to her:

"Everyone who drinks this water will be thirsty again, but those who drink the water that I will give them, will never be thirsty. The water that I will give will become a spring of water gushing up to eternal life."

The woman said to him:

"Sir, give me this water."

Then she went back to her town and told everyone about her conversation with Jesus.

From the Gospel of John,
chapter 4, verses 1 to 24.

What is the living water which Jesus speaks of?

Water is essential for life, and people are most aware of this in a hot desert country. Water quenches thirst, and washes clean. So water is a symbol of life, and water brings the life of God in baptism. The Holy Spirit is also spoken of as living water.

The Lord of the sea

Was Jesus a magician?

No. Jesus is far more powerful than a magician. The storm at sea represents unknown dangers in the world, and powerful forces which could lead to death. Jesus is more powerful than any forces that may try to harm us. All evil powers can be overcome in the name of Jesus.

One day Jesus and his disciples left the crowds and took a boat to cross the sea of Galilee. But a violent storm arose, and the waves were coming into the boat. Jesus was asleep. The disciples shouted at him:

"Master, do you not care that we are drowning?"

Jesus woke up and rebuked the wind, and said to the sea:

"Peace, be still!"

Then the wind ceased, and there was a dead calm. He said to them:

"Why are you so afraid? Have you still no faith?"

They were filled with awe, and said to one another:

"Who is Jesus? Even the wind and the sea obey him."

From the Gospel of Mark,
chapter 4, verses 35 to 41.

Feeding the thousands

One day such a huge crowd gathered around Jesus and his disciples that they did not even have time to eat. So Jesus said:

"Let's go across to the other side of the lake to rest."

They set off in the boat, but when they arrived at the other side a huge crowd was already waiting for them there. When Jesus saw them, like a flock of sheep without a shepherd, he was sorry for them and he talked to them for a long time. The disciples were worried:

"It's late," they said, "let them go and find something to eat."

But Jesus answered:

"You give them something to eat."

"It would be too expensive to get food for all these people," said the disciples.

"How many loaves do you have? Go and see," said Jesus.

The disciples checked, and said:

"Five loaves and two small fishes."

Did Jews usually bless bread before eating it?

Yes. This is a Jewish custom which Jesus followed. At the last supper Jesus broke bread and blessed it, and we remember this in our worship today.

Jesus told the people to sit down in groups of fifty or a hundred people. He took the loaves and the fishes, and looking up to heaven he blessed them, broke them up and gave them to the disciples to distribute. Everyone ate as much as they wanted, and when the disciples collected what was left over, there were twelve baskets full. Five thousand people had been fed.

From the Gospel of Mark, chapter 6, verses 30 to 44.

Who is Jesus?

Jesus and his disciples were going from one village to another. On the way he asked them:

"Who do people say I am?"

"John the Baptist, or Elijah, or another prophet," the disciples replied.

"But who do you say that I am?" Jesus asked.

Peter answered:

"You are the Christ, the Messiah."

Jesus ordered them to tell no one about him. Then he began to teach them that he would undergo great suffering, and be rejected by the religious leaders, and be killed, and after three days rise again.

Peter took him aside and reproached him for saying such things. But Jesus turned and looked at his disciples and said to Peter:

"You are talking like the devil. You are not thinking in God's way, but in a human way."

From the Gospel of Mark,
chapter 8, verses 27 to 33.

How did Jesus know that he was going to die and rise again?

Jesus could see that the religious leaders hated him and that his life was in danger. But his faith in God made him believe that God would overcome death and raise him up.

What is the meaning of the words 'Christ' and 'Messiah'?

They are the same word: 'Christ' comes from a Greek word and 'Messiah' from a Hebrew word, meaning 'the one who has been anointed with holy oil'. Kings were anointed with this oil, and the Jews were waiting for a special king, sent by God.

The transfiguration of Jesus

What is the meaning of this story?

First you need to remember the story of Moses shining with God's light on Mount Sinai. Jesus has gone up the mountain, like Moses, to be with God, and Jesus is the Son of God. For Peter, James and John this discovery is a miracle.

Six days later, Jesus took Peter, James and John up a high mountain. Suddenly he was transfigured in front of them, and his clothes became dazzling white. Then his disciples saw him talking with Moses and Elijah. Then Peter said to Jesus:

"Rabbi, it is good that we are here. Let us make three huts, one for you, one for Moses and one for Elijah."

In fact Peter did not know what to say, because they were so astonished. A cloud covered the disciples and they heard a voice, saying:

"This is my beloved Son, listen to him!"

Suddenly when they looked round, they saw noone else there, but Jesus alone.

From the Gospel of Mark, chapter 9, verses 2 to 8.

Jesus and the children

People were bringing little children to Jesus, but the disciples stopped them. When Jesus saw this he was angry and said to them:

"Let the children come to me, and do not stop them. The kingdom of God belongs to children and to people like them. I tell you, whoever does not receive the kingdom of God as a little child will never enter it."

Jesus picked up the children in his arms, and put his hands on them and blessed them.

From the Gospel of Mark,
chapter 10, verses 13 to 16.

Why did the disciples stop the children coming near to Jesus?

In those days people thought children were not important. But Jesus welcomed them and told adults to follow the example of children: by being trusting and open.

The good Samaritan

Why did the priest and the Levite not stop?

Because they had religious duties to do, and they believed that touching a corpse would make them impure. So they were making their religious rules more important than helping someone in trouble.

A lawyer asked Jesus:
"Who is my neighbour?"
Jesus told him this parable:
"A man was travelling from Jerusalem to Jericho, and was attacked by robbers, who beat him up, stole his money and ran away, leaving him half dead. A priest from the temple came past: he saw him and crossed the road to avoid him. Later a Levite came along, and went by on the other side.

But a Samaritan, who was passing through the area, came upon the wounded man, and was moved with pity. He went to him and bandaged his wounds, and put him on his own donkey and took him to an inn.

The next day, he gave the innkeeper some money and said:

"Take care of him, and if you spend more, I will repay you when I come back."
Then Jesus asked the lawyer:
"Which of these three people was a good neighbour to the man who was attacked by robbers?"

"The one who showed him mercy," replied the lawyer.

Jesus said to him:
"Go and do the same."

From the Gospel of Luke, chapter 10, verses 29 to 37.

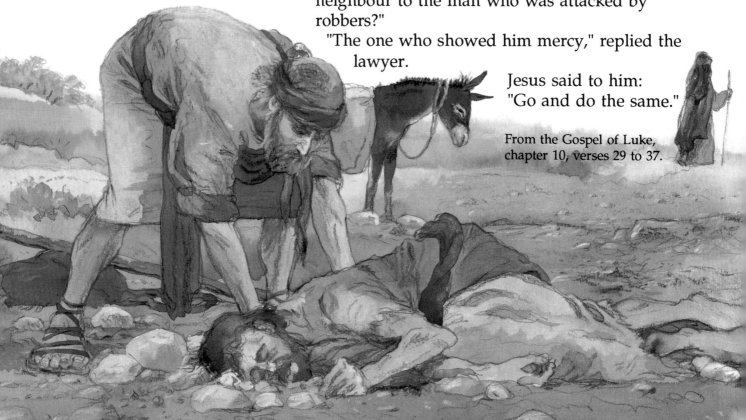

The lost sheep

Some people who did not keep the religious laws came to hear Jesus. And the religious leaders protested at this:

"This man receives sinners, and eats with them," they said.

Then Jesus told this parable:

"If one of you has a hundred sheep and loses one, what does he do? He leaves the ninety-nine sheep, and goes to look for the one that is lost. When he finds it, he is delighted. He puts it on his shoulders and brings it back home, and he tells all his friends and neighbours so they can share his joy.

I tell you: God is more delighted at one sinner who asks forgiveness, than at ninety-nine good people who do not need forgiveness."

From the Gospel of Luke, chapter 15, verses 1 to 7.

Why did religious leaders protest about what Jesus did?

They thought that their religion taught them to keep away from sinners in case they might sin too. They were shocked that Jesus made friends with sinners and went to their houses.

The prodigal son

Jesus told this parable:

A man had two sons. The younger one said to his father: "Let me have my share of the money you will leave us." The father gave him his share, and a few days later, the younger son packed up his possessions, and went away to a distant country. There he spent all the money, leading a wild life. Soon there was a famine in that area, and he had nothing left. So he took a job looking after pigs. He would gladly have eaten the pig food, and no one gave him anything.

So he thought:

"How many of my father's farm-workers have food enough and to spare, but here I am dying of hunger. I will go back to my father and ask his forgiveness."

That is what he did. While he was still far off, his father saw him coming and was filled with compassion: he ran towards him and put his arms around him and kissed him. The younger son said:

"Father, I have sinned against heaven and before you, and I am no more worthy to be called your son . . . "

But the father said to the servants:

"Quick, bring out the best robe for him, and kill a fatted calf and let us celebrate! This son of mine was dead, and is alive again; he was lost, and now he's found."

And they began the feast. But when the elder brother came back from his work in the fields he asked what was happening. One of the servants said:

"Your father is celebrating the return of your brother."

The elder son was very angry with his father. He said:

"For all these years I have been working for you, and I have never disobeyed you, and yet you've never given me such a feast. But now this son of yours has come back, after wasting all your money, and you have killed the fatted calf for him."

The father replied:

"Son, you are always with me, and all that I have is yours. But your brother was dead, and is alive again; he was lost and is found."

From the Gospel of Luke,
chapter 15, verses 11 to 32.

The little man
in the tree

Jesus was going through the town of Jericho. A man called Zacchaeus wanted to see him. He was the chief tax collector and he was very rich. As he was small he could not see over the heads of the crowd, so he ran ahead and climbed a tree. When Jesus arrived, he looked up at Zacchaeus and said:

"Zacchaeus, come down quickly! I want to visit your house today!"

Zacchaeus came down from the tree and was delighted to entertain Jesus. But when people saw this they muttered:

"Jesus has gone to visit a sinner."

But Zacchaeus stood there and said to Jesus:

"Look, Lord, I'll give half my property to the poor. And if I've cheated anyone, I will give him four times as much in compensation."

Jesus said:

"Today salvation has come to this house. I came to seek out and save the lost."

From the Gospel of Luke,
chapter 19, verses 1 to 10.

Blind Bartimaeus

Jesus was leaving Jericho with his disciples, followed by a large crowd. A blind beggar, called Bartimaeus, was sitting beside the road. When he heard that Jesus was coming he started to call out:
"Jesus, Son of David, have mercy on me!"
People told him to keep quiet, but he only shouted louder:
"Son of David, have mercy on me!"
Jesus stopped and said:
"Call him over here."
So they called the beggar:
"Take heart, get up; he is calling you."
The beggar threw off his cloak, sprang up and came to Jesus. Jesus asked him:
"What do you want me to do for you?"
"Lord, I would like to see again," he said.
Jesus said to him:
"Go. Your faith has made you well."
Immediately Bartimaeus recovered his sight, and followed Jesus.

From the Gospel of Mark,
chapter 10, verses 46 to 52.

How far did Bartimaeus follow Jesus?

We do not know. Jesus was on his way to Jerusalem. Bartimaeus believed in him and followed him to Jerusalem, to his death and resurrection. We are also invited to follow Jesus from death to life.

Triumph in Jerusalem

*Why did Jesus ride
a donkey?*

*In Jesus' days, horses
were used for war, and
donkeys for peaceful
work. By riding a
donkey Jesus showed
he was the Prince of
Peace foretold by the
prophets.*

Jesus and his disciples were travelling to
Jerusalem, and they had reached Bethany and the
Mount of Olives. Jesus sent two disciples ahead,
with these instructions:

"Go to the village opposite. You will find a
young donkey, whom no one had yet ridden, tied
up. Bring it here. If anyone asks what you are
doing, say that the Lord needs the donkey, and
will send it back."

The disciples did what Jesus had told them, and
no one interfered. They brought the donkey back,
and covered it with their coats, and Jesus sat on
it. Crowds of people spread their coats and palm
branches on the road. And those who were
walking along shouted:

"Hosanna! Blessed is he who comes in the name
of the Lord! Hosanna in the highest!"

Jesus went into the temple at Jerusalem. He
looked around, and then, as it was evening, he
went back to Bethany with his disciples.

From the Gospel of Mark,
chapter 11, verses 1 to 11.

Panic in the temple

Why were people selling things in the temple?

To supply animals for sacrifices to the worshippers, and to change money for the pilgrims.

The next day, Jesus went back to Jerusalem; he went into the temple and drove out all the buyers and sellers who were there. He tipped over the table of the money-changers, and the chairs of the pigeon-sellers and he would not let anyone go through the temple with their goods. Then he said:
"Our holy books say: 'My house shall be called the house of prayer

for all the peoples.' But you have made it a den of thieves."

The religious leaders and teachers heard what Jesus had done, and discussed how they could stop him. They were afraid of him, because the people admired him and listened to him.

From the Gospel of Mark,
chapter 11, verses 15 to 18.

A woman condemned to death

Why did Jesus not condemn this woman?

Jesus did not approve of what she had done. But he thought it was better to help her to change her attitude and her way of life, rather than punish her.

One day some religious leaders, who wanted to test Jesus, brought a woman to him, and said:

"Rabbi, this woman was caught in bed with a man who is not her husband. The law of Moses tells us to stone her to death. What do you say?"

Jesus bent over and drew something with his finger in the sand, but they went on asking him. In the end he said:

"Let the person who has never sinned throw the first stone."

Then he leaned over again to write in the sand. When they heard his reply, the people went away, one after another, starting with the oldest. Only the woman was left, alone with Jesus. Jesus asked her:

"Where are your accusers? Has no one condemned you?"

"No one, sir."

"Neither do I condemn you. Go, and do not do it again."

From the Gospel of John, chapter 8, verses 3 to 11.

Lazarus comes back to life

While Jesus was away from Judea with his disciples, he heard that his friend Lazarus was very ill. But he did not return to Judea until two days later, and by then Lazarus was dead. Jesus said to his disciples:

"Our friend Lazarus is asleep. I must go and wake him."

When Jesus arrived, Lazarus had already been in the tomb for four days. Lazarus' sisters, Martha and Mary were surrounded by people. Martha came to meet Jesus.

"Lord," she said, "if you had been here, Lazarus wouldn't have died. But even now I know that God will grant you whatever you ask."

Jesus replied:

"Your brother will come back to life. I am the resurrection and the life. Whoever lives and believes in me will never die."

Martha said:

"Yes, Lord, I believe that you are the Christ, the Son of God, who was to come into the world."

Mary also came to him and fell at his feet, weeping, and said:

"Lord, if you had been here, our brother would not have died."

Jesus was overcome, and he wept too.

Was the resurrection of Lazarus like the resurrection of Jesus?

No. When Jesus rose from the dead he conquered death once and for all. The resurrection of Lazarus brought him back to life for a time, but it pointed ahead to Jesus' resurrection.

When they reached the tomb, Jesus asked the people to roll away the stone and he prayed:

"Father, I thank you because you have heard my prayer. You always hear me, but I said this so that the crowd here may believe that you sent me."

Then he shouted in a loud voice:

"Lazarus! Come out!"

And Lazarus, who had been dead, came out.

Many of those who were standing by believed in Jesus. But when the religious leaders heard about it, they held a meeting and said:

"If we let him go on like this, everyone will believe in him, and the Romans will come and destroy our temple and our nation." From that day on, they planned to put him to death.

From the Gospel of John,
chapter 11, verses 1 to 53.

Judas betrays Jesus

Two days before the feast of the Passover, the religious leaders were trying to find a way to arrest and execute Jesus. They said to each other:

"We must not arrest him during the feast, or the people will be angry."

Judas came to them, and offered to betray Jesus to them at a time and place where no one would see. They were very pleased and promised him thirty pieces of silver. Judas now began to look out for a suitable moment to betray Jesus.

From the Gospel of Mark,
chapter 14, verses 1 to 2
and 10 to 11.

Why did Judas betray Jesus?

No one knows for certain. Possibly he was disillusioned about Jesus. Or possibly he was tempted by the money. The gospels say he was overcome by evil.

The last supper

Did Jesus really mean people to eat his body and drink his blood?

No. By repeating the actions and words of Jesus, eating the bread and drinking the wine, Christians can really share in the death and resurrection of Jesus.

On the first day of the Passover Jesus' disciples went in to Jerusalem to prepare the room for the Passover meal. In the evening, Jesus arrived with the twelve apostles. At the beginning of the meal he told them:

"One of you is going to betray me."

They were all distressed and asked him one by one:

"Lord, is it I?"

"It is one of the twelve who is dipping his bread in the dish with me," said Jesus. "But woe to the man who betrays the Son of Man. It would be better for him if he had never been born."

While they were eating, Jesus took a loaf of bread, blessed it and broke it, and gave it to them, saying:

"Take, eat, this is my body."

Then he took a cup, and after giving thanks he gave it to them, and all of them drank from it. He said to them:

"This is my blood of the covenant, which is poured out for many. I tell you, I will never again drink of the fruit of the vine until that day when I drink it new in the kingdom of God."

When they had sung a hymn, they went out. Jesus said to them:

"You will all desert me."

Peter said:

"Even though all the others desert you, I never will."

Jesus replied:

"Truly, I tell you, this very might, before the cock crows twice, you will deny me three times."

But Peter insisted:

"Even if I have to die with you, I will not deny you." And all of them said the same.

From the Gospel of Mark,
chapter 14, verses 12 to 31.

Arrested at night

Jesus did not want to answer violence with more violence. He gave his life so that people might learn that only love of others leads to eternal life.

Jesus and his disciples went to Gethsemane, a garden of olive trees, and Jesus asked his disciples to stay awake while he prayed. He threw himself on the ground and prayed that if it were possible the hour might pass from him:

"Father, I am afraid to die, but I have faith in you. Let your will be done, not mine."

He came back and found the apostles sleeping, and said to Peter:

"Could you not stay awake with me for one hour?"

Then Judas arrived, with a crowd of men armed with swords and sticks, sent by the religious leaders. Judas had told them:

"The one I will kiss is the man; arrest him and lead him away under guard."

Judas went straight up to Jesus, said "Rabbi!" and kissed him. Then the guards seized Jesus, and Jesus said to them:

"Have you come out with swords and clubs to arrest me, as if I were a bandit? Day after day I was with you in the temple teaching, and you did not arrest me."

Then all the disciples deserted him and fled.

From the Gospel of Mark, chapter 14, verses 32 to 50.

Peter's denial

The guards took Jesus to the High Priest's palace. Peter and another disciple followed them. As this disciple knew the High Priest, they were both able to enter the courtyard, where the servants had lit a fire to keep themselves warm. A servant girl said to Peter:

"Aren't you another of this man's disciples?"

"No, I'm not," said Peter.

Meanwhile the High Priest was questioning Jesus about his disciples and his teaching. Jesus answered:

"I have spoken openly to the world; I have always taught in synagogues and in the temple. I have said nothing in secret. Why do you ask me? Ask those who heard what I said to them; they know what I said."

One of the guards struck Jesus in the face, saying:

"Is that how you answer the High Priest?"

Jesus answered:

"If I have spoken wrongly, give evidence of this; if not, why do you hit me?"

In the courtyad Peter was warming himself at the fire. Someone said to him:

"You aren't also one of his disciples, are you?"

Peter denied this.

"Surely I saw you in the garden with him?" said another.

"No," said Peter again. And the cock crowed.

From the Gospel of John,
chapter 18, verses 13 to 27.

Jesus is questioned

What were the Romans doing in Jesus' country?

They had occupied the country for about a hundred years. They allowed the Jews to practise their religion, but the Romans controlled the government and only they had the right to execute criminals.

At dawn, Jesus was brought before Pilate, the Roman governor. The religious leader stayed outside the palace. Pilate came out to ask them:

"What accusation do you bring against this man?"

"He is an evildoer" they said. Pilate said:

"Then take him and judge him according to your law."

"But," they said, "we have no right to put anyone to death."

So Pilate went back in and asked Jesus:

"Are you the king of the Jews?"

Jesus answered:

"Do you ask this on your own, or did others tell you about me?"

"I am not a Jew," said Pilate, "your own nation and the chief priests have handed you over to me. What have you done?"

"My kingdom is not from this world," Jesus replied. "If it were my followers would be fighting to defend me."

"So you are a king?" asked Pilate.

"You say that I am a king," said Jesus. "I came into the world, to witness to the truth."

"What is truth?" said Pilate.

From the Gospel of John, chapter 18, verses 28 to 38

Sentenced to be crucified

Then he went out to the Jews again and told them:

"I find no case against him. But you have a custom that I release someone for you at the Passover. Do you want me to release the king of the Jews?"

"No," they shouted, "not this man, but Barabbas."

Now Barabbas was a bandit.

Pilate had Jesus beaten. The soldiers put a royal robe on him and a crown of thorns on his head and mocked him, saying:

"Hail, King of the Jews!"

They hit him in the face. Pilate then took him out to the religious leaders and said:

"Here is the man."

When they saw him they shouted:

"Crucify him! Crucify him!"

Pilate told them that he found no case against him. But they answered:

"We have a law, and by that law he ought to die, because he claimed to be the Son of God. If you release this man, you are no friend of Caesar."

Finally Pilate handed over Jesus to be crucified. It was a Friday, the day before the Passover Sabbath, about noon.

From the Gospel of John, chapter 18, verse 39 to chapter 19, verse 16.

Why was it an offence worthy of death, to claim to be the Son of God?

The Jews believed that God was one and far above humans. So if someone dared to say "I am the Son of God", he would be claiming to be equal to God. This was a terrible thing in the eyes of the Jews.

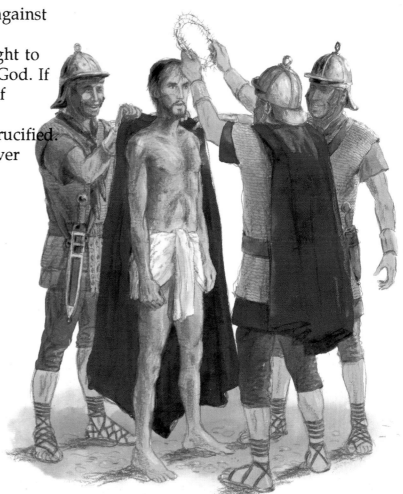

Jesus is crucified

Were people condemned to death always crucified?

No. Crucifixion was used only for slaves, and for those who were not Roman citizens, as a punishment for murder, theft, treason and rebellion. It was a horrible torture, which could last several days.

Jesus carried his cross to Golgotha, outside the city. There they crucified him, and with him two others, one on each side. Pilate had an inscription written, and nailed on the cross. It read:

"Jesus of Nazareth, the King of the Jews."

The soldiers divided his clothes into four parts, one for each soldier, and they cast lots for his tunic, which was woven in one piece.

When Jesus saw his mother and the disciple he loved, standing at the foot of the cross, he said to them:

"Woman, here is your son." And to the disciple:

"Here is your mother."

Then he said:

"It is finished." And he bowed his head and gave up his spirit.

Since it was Friday, and they did not want the bodies to be on the crosses on the Sabbath day, the religious leaders asked Pilate to have them removed. So the soldiers broke the legs of the others, but when they found that Jesus was already dead, they did not break his legs, but pierced his side with a spear, and at once blood and water came out.

Pilate allowed Joseph of Arimathea, a follower of Jesus, to take away the body, and Nicodemus, another follower, brought myrrh and aloes to embalm the body. They wrapped Jesus in a linen cloth and put him in a new tomb in a garden near where he was crucified.

From the Gospel of John,
chapter 19, verses 17 to 41.

Jesus is alive!

What proofs are there of the resurrection?

No one saw the resurrection of Jesus. But the disciples often saw Jesus after he rose again, and were astonished by this unexpected event. Ever since, Christians have believed their word. And many people have chosen to die rather than give up their belief that Jesus rose again.

On the first day of the week, while it was still dark, Mary Magdalene came to the tomb and saw that the stone, which had been rolled in front of the door of the tomb, had been removed. She ran to Simon Peter and the other disciple, and said:

"They have taken the Lord out of the tomb, and we do not know where they have laid him."

The disciples ran to the tomb; the other disciple got there first and saw the linen cloths, but he did not go in. Peter went in and saw the linen cloths, and the cloth that had been on Jesus' head lying separately. Then they both believed; till then they had not understood the scripture, that the Christ must rise from the dead. Then they went home.

Mary stood weeping by the tomb; she turned round and Jesus was there, though she did not recognize him. He asked her:

"Why are you weeping?"

She thought he was the gardener, and said:

"Sir, tell me where he is, and I will take him away."

Jesus said to her: "Mary!"

Suddenly she recognized him: "Master!"

Jesus said to her:

"Do not hold on to me. But go and tell my brothers that I am going to my Father and yours, to my God and your God."

Mary went and told the disciples:

"I have seen the Lord," and she told them what Jesus had said.

From the Gospel of John,
chapter 20, verses 1 to 18.

Thomas asks for proof

What is the Holy Spirit?

The Greek word for "spirit" also means "breath". God sends his holy "breath" to breathe his love into our hearts and bring us to life.

That very day, Jesus appeared to the disciples together, showed them the wounds in his hands and his side, and the disciples were full of joy.

"Peace be with you," said Jesus, "as the Father has sent me, so I send you."

Then he breathed on them and said:

"Receive the Holy Spirit. If you forgive the sins of anyone they are forgiven; if you do not, they are not forgiven."

The disciples told Thomas what had happened, because he was not there, but he would not believe them.

A week later, Jesus appeared again.

"Peace be with you," he said, "Thomas, come here:

look at my hands, and put your hand in my side. Do not doubt, but believe."

Thomas answered him:

"My Lord and my God!"

Jesus said to him:

"Because you have seen you have believed. Blessed are those who have not seen, and yet have come to believe."

From the Gospel of John, chapter 20, verses 19 to 29.

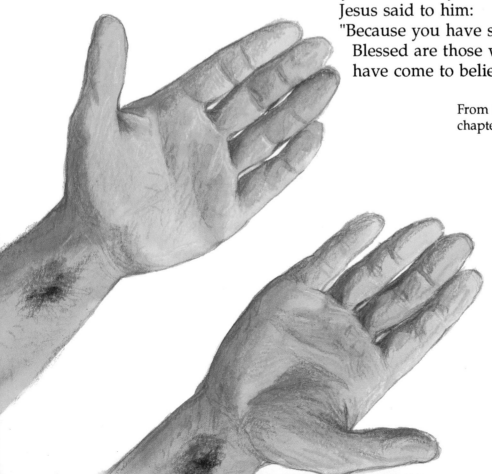

On the road to Emmaus

The same day, two disciples were walking sadly towards their village, Emmaus. Jesus came along and walked beside them, but they did not recognize him. Jesus asked them:

"What are you talking about?"

One of them, called Cleopas, replied:

"Are you the only person who does not know what has been happening this week? Jesus of Nazareth, a prophet before God and the people, was crucified by the religious leaders and the Romans three days ago. And we were hoping that he would save our country. And today some women have amazed us: they went to the tomb and Jesus' body was gone, and an angel told them that Jesus was alive. Some disciples went to the tomb, but they did not see him."

Jesus said to them:

"How slow you are to believe all the prophets foretold!"

And he explained to them all the prophecies about him from the Old Testament. When they arrived at Emmaus, the disciples said to Jesus:

"Stay with us, because it is nearly evening."

Why did the disciples not recognize Jesus?

The disciples were trying so hard to find Jesus as they had known him before, that they did not recognize him when he joined them. But as they heard God's word and shared the bread they saw the new, risen face of Jesus, which can only be seen with the eyes of faith.

When Jesus was at supper with them he took bread, blessed it and broke it and gave it to them. Suddenly their eyes were opened and they recognized him, but he disappeared. They said to each other:

"Were not our hearts burning within us while he was talking to us on the road?"

They immediately returned to Jerusalem to see the apostles, who told them:

"It's true. The Lord is risen indeed!"

The two disciples then told what had happened to them on the way, and how they had recognized Jesus when he broke the bread.

From the Gospel of Luke,
chapter 24, verses 13 to 35.

Jesus goes to his Father

Jesus told his disciples not to leave Jerusalem, but to wait there for the promise of the Father. He said:

"You will be baptized with the Holy Spirit not many days from now."

The disciples asked:

"Lord, are you now going to restore the kingdom to Israel?"

Jesus replied:

"It is not for you to know the times when God will act. But you will receive power, when the Holy Spirit has come, and you will be my witnesses, in Judea and Samaria and to the ends of the earth."

As they were watching he was lifted up, and disappeared into a cloud. They were still looking up into the sky when two men in white appeared and said:

"Why do you stand looking towards heaven? Jesus will come again in the same way as you saw him go into heaven."

From the Acts of the Apostles,
chapter 1, verses 4 to 11.

How did Jesus leave?

The ascension into heaven is a way of showing that the risen Jesus belonged to God, and could no longer be seen on earth.

The wind of Pentecost

How could the disciples suddenly make themselves understood in foreign languages?

The story of Pentecost shows the effect of the Holy Spirit. Just as human beings stopped understanding each other at Babel (see page 22), now, thanks to the Spirit, they could understand each other, even if they did not speak the same language.

Fifty days after Passover, Jesus' disciples met to celebrate the Jewish feast of Pentecost. Suddenly they heard a sound like the rush of a violent wind, and they saw tongues of fire over each of them. All of them were filled with the Holy Spirit and began to speak in other languages.

Now there were Jews from every nation living in Jerusalem, and they were amazed at what was happening:

"Are not all these people who are speaking Galileans?" they asked. "How is it that we can all understand in our own languages?"

And others said:

"They are filled with new wine."

Peter spoke to them:

"No," he said, "we are not drunk. Today the prophecy, 'I will pour out my Spirit' has come true. You made the Romans crucify Jesus of Nazareth. But God has raised him up, and we are witnesses. God has made him the Christ, and Lord of all."

The people listened to Peter and were moved.
They asked the disciples:
"Brothers, what must we do?"
Peter replied:
"Repent and be baptized every one of you in the
name of Jesus Christ, so that your sins may be
forgiven. Then you will receive the gift of the
Holy Spirit."
On that day about three thousand people
were baptized and joined the disciples.

From the Acts of the Apostles,
chapter 2, verses 1 to 41.

Brothers and sisters

*Were the first Christians
so perfect?*

*This passage from the
Acts of the Apostles
shows the ideal church
community. But elsewhere
in the book it is clear that
there were problems.
It needs continual
effort to live a perfect life.*

Jesus' new disciples faithfully followed the
teaching of the apostles. They lived together in
fellowship; they sold all their possessions and
shared the money with everyone, according to
each person's needs. Every day they went to pray
in the temple. They praised God and broke bread
in memory of Jesus, and all the people thought
well of them. And day by day the Lord added to
their number those who were being saved.

From the Acts of the Apostles,
chapter 2, verses 42 to 47.

Two apostles arrested
in the temple

One day, Peter and John were going to the temple to pray, and a man lame from birth was begging for money. Peter looked intently at him and said:

"Look at us. We have no silver or gold, but what we have we give you: in the name of Jesus Christ, stand up and walk!"

Immediately the lame man was cured. He went into the temple with them, praising God. The people recognized him, and they were filled with wonder. Peter explained to them that they had done this miracle in the name of Jesus, and told them about Jesus' resurrection, and asked them to repent, and change their way of life.

The religious leaders were furious, and had the two apostles arrested, and ordered them not to speak or to teach at all in the name of Jesus. But Peter and John replied:

"What should we do: obey you, or obey God? We cannot keep from speaking about what we have seen and heard."

The religious leaders had to let them go for fear of the people, and because they could find no good reason to condemn them.

From the Acts of the Apostles,
chapter 3, and chapter 4,
verses 1 to 21.

Stephen is stoned

Who was Stephen?

Stephen was chosen to be a deacon, with six other disciples; their job was with Greek-speaking Christians in Jerusalem, especially the widows and the poor. He was also responsible for the community meals and for preaching. When he died for his faith he became the first ever Christian martyr.

Stephen was a disciple full of God's power, and he performed miracles and signs in God's name. One day a group of Jews had an argument with Stephen, and when they could not win the argument they stirred up the people and the religious leaders against Stephen, and had him arrested and brought into court. They accused him:

"This man speaks against the law and the temple. He says that Jesus will destroy the temple and change the law of Moses."

The judges looked intently at Stephen, and they saw that his face was like the face of an angel. Stephen told them the whole history of Israel, and showed how Jesus was the Messiah the Jews were waiting for.

These words made them very angry. They rushed at him and dragged him out of the city and stoned him to death. A young man called Paul was looking after their clothes. As the stones hit him, Stephen prayed:

"Lord Jesus, receive my spirit."
Then, falling on his knees he shouted aloud:
"Lord, do not hold this sin against them."
When he had said this, he died.

From the Acts of the Apostles,
chapter 6, verses 8 to 15, and
chapter 7.

Paul's experience
on the road to Damascus

Paul hated the disciples of Jesus and wanted to arrest them all. He was on his way to Damascus to arrest the disciples there.

On the way, a light from heaven flashed around him. He fell to the ground and heard a voice:

"Paul, why do you persecute me?"

"Who are you, Lord?" asked Paul.

"I am Jesus, whom you are persecuting. Get up and enter the city, and wait to hear what you must do."

Paul got up, but he was blind, so they led him by the hand to Damascus. For three days he was blind, and neither ate nor drank.

The Lord called Ananias, one of his disciples who lived in Damascus:

"Ananias, get up and go to a man named Paul. At the moment he is praying."

"Lord," said Ananias, "I have heard of all the harm he has done to our brothers and sisters in Jerusalem. And he has come here to arrest all those who follow you."

"Go," said the Lord, "for he is the one I have chosen to bring my name to the whole world."

Ananias went to Paul, and laid hands on him:

"Brother Paul," he said, "the Lord Jesus, has sent me to you. Receive your sight, and be filled with the Holy Spirit."

At once, Paul recovered his sight, and then he was baptized. He ate some food, and regained his strength. He went to all the synagogues and proclaimed that Jesus was the Son of God.

From the Acts of the Apostles,
chapter 9, verses 1 to 20.

Paul's travels for God

How did Paul die?

The Acts of the Apostles does not say. The book ends with Paul's arrival in Rome: this is when the gospel reaches the capital of the known world. Later it is said that Paul was executed in Rome at the same time as Peter, about AD 63.

Some years later, a disciple called Barnabas asked Paul to go with him to preach the gospel in Antioch, a great city in Syria. Then these two disciples were chosen to go on a mission to Asia Minor. They began by speaking to the Jews in the synagogues, but they were often driven out of the synagogues, and went to preach to the pagans. They went from town to town, and from country to country, led by the Holy Spirit.

After this first mission, Paul made another journey to preach the gospel of Jesus as far away as Greece. When he returned to Jerusalem, some people, who were angry that he had been preaching the gospel, had him arrested. But because he was a Roman citizen, Paul was able to appeal to Caesar and go to Rome for trial.

The ship in which Paul was travelling was wrecked, but Paul arrived safely in Rome three months later. In Rome he gained the support of many of the Jewish leaders, and many came to hear him teach. Paul spoke of the Kingdom of God, and from morning till night he taught about Jesus.

From the Acts of the Apostles, chapters 13 to 28.

The voyages of Paul

1st voyage
2nd voyage
3rd voyage
4th voyage

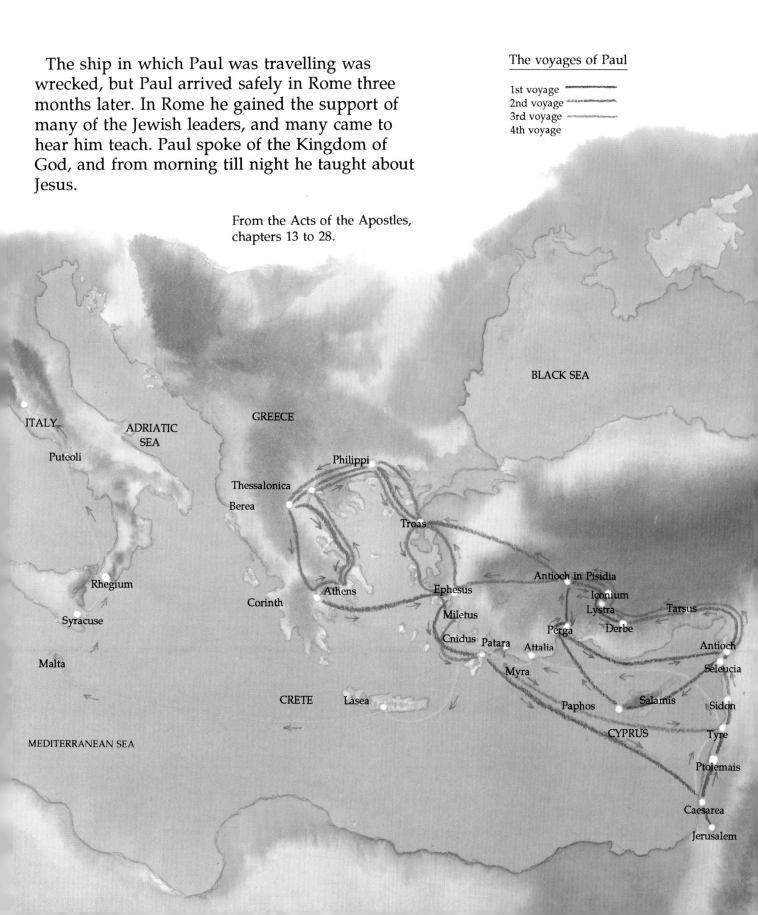

BLACK SEA

ITALY
ADRIATIC SEA
GREECE
Puteoli
Philippi
Thessalonica
Berea
Troas
Antioch in Pisidia
Rhegium
Athens
Ephesus
Iconium
Lystra
Tarsus
Corinth
Miletus
Perga
Derbe
Syracuse
Cnidus
Patara
Attalia
Antioch
Malta
Myra
Seleucia
CRETE
Lasea
Paphos
Salamis
Sidon
MEDITERRANEAN SEA
CYPRUS
Tyre
Ptolemais
Caesarea
Jerusalem

If I have no love

Paul regularly wrote letters (called epistles) to the Christian communities he had founded, during his missionary journeys. Here is a passage from one of his best letters, which he sent to Christians in the town of Corinth, in Greece, around AD 56:

"If I speak in the tongues of humans and of angels, but have no love, I am a noisy gong or a clashing cymbal.

If I know all about God, and understand all mysteries, and have no love, I am nothing.

If I give away all my possessions, but have no love, I gain nothing.

Love is patient; love is kind; love is not envious or boastful or arrogant or rude. Love does not insist on its own way; it is not irritable or resentful; it does not rejoice in wrongdoing, but rejoices in the truth.

Love bears all things, believes all things, hopes all things, endures all things.

Love never ends."

From the First Letter of Paul
to the Corinthians, chapter 13,
verses 1 to 13.

150

Six Questions
on the Bible

1. What is in the Bible?

The word Bible means book. And in fact the Bible is a library of books. The Jewish Bible (the Torah) consists of over forty books. The Christian Bible is divided into two parts: the Old Testament and the New Testament.

The Old Testament includes the books of the Jewish Bible. Most of these were written in Hebrew, but some were written in Greek. Some Christians include all these books in the Old Testament, while others only count the 39 books which were written in Hebrew; they call the ones in Greek "The Apocrypha". There are two stories from the Apocrypha in the Old Testament part of this Bible: they are on pages 70 and 74.

The New Testament includes twenty seven books: among them are the four Gospels ("gospel" means "good news"). Each Gospel tells in its own way what Jesus said and did.

2. When was the Bible written?

The oldest parts of the Bible were not written down at first. They were told to children by their parents. Then, about three thousand years ago people started writing them down. The newest parts are about 1900 years old.

3. Who wrote the Bible?

Believers say the Bible is the Word of God. This doesn't mean that God actually wrote it word for word.

Human beings wrote it: they were the authors of the Bible even though some of them are unknown to us. But Jews and Christians believe that God inspired them to try to give us answers to the great questions of life: "Who are we?" "Where did we come from?" "Who is God?" "Why is there evil and death in the world?"

4. What does the Bible tell us?

All sorts of things. There are adventure stories, history, stories of amusing or strange happenings, worship songs (called "Psalms"), love poems, advice on how to live, proverbs, letters . . . But in all these different ways, the Bible is telling us above all, how God loves the human race.

5. Who reads the Bible these days?

These days millions of men and women read the Bible, throughout the whole world. It's the world's best seller: it has been translated into 1928 languages, and an estimated 2.5 billion copies have been printed since 1815!

Christians read the Bible every day, and especially on Sunday when they meet for worship. Together they try to understand what God is saying to them.

And many people of other religions, or of no religion at all, also read the Bible.

6. Is all of the Bible in this book?

No, the Bible is too big, and some of it is difficult to read and understand. So we have chosen some of the best stories and told them clearly, without spoiling them.

To help you understand there are questions and answers beside the stories.

We hope that reading this book will make you want to go on and read more of the Bible, to discover the rest of its riches.

The authors

Index of names
of people and places

A

Aaron: 38, 40, 46

Abednego: 79

Abel: 17

Abraham: 23 to 26, 49, 54

Adam: 17

Ananias: 144

Andrew: 94, 144

Anna: 57

Antioch: 146

Antiochus: 79

Asia Minor: 146

Augustus Caesar: 89

B

Babel: 22, 138

Babylon: 23, 68, 69, 70, 79

Balthasar: 91

Barabbas: 129

Barnabas: 146

Bartholomew: 94

Bartimaeus: 115

Benjamin: 31, 32, 33

Bethany: 116

Bethlehem: 59, 89, 90, 91

Bethulia: 70, 71

C

Cain: 17

Cana: 96

Canaan: 23, 27, 31, 32, 34, 37, 49, 54, 55

Capernaum: 97

Caspar: 91

Corinth: 148

Cyrus: 69

D

Damascus: 144

Daniel: 80, 81

Darius: 80, 81

David: 59 to 68, 85, 88

Dead Sea: 31

Delilah: 55

E

Egypt: 28 to 32, 34, 37 to 40, 44 to 46, 49, 68, 93

Eli: 57

Eliab: 59

Elijah: 107, 108

Emmaus: 135

Esther: 72, 73

Eve: 17

Ezekiel: 78

G

Gabriel: 88

Galilee: 88, 94, 138

Gethsemane: (see Mount of Olives)

Golgotha: 130

Goliath: 60

Goshen: 31, 34, 40, 42

Greece: 146, 148

H

Haman: 72, 73

Haran: 23

Hebron: 31

Herod: 91

Hiram: 67

Holophernes: 70, 71

I

Isaac: 25 to 27, 49

Isaiah: 78, 85

Israel: 35, 49, 50, 137, 142

J

Jacob: 27, 28, 31 to 35, 49, 54, 103

James: 94, 95, 108

Jehoiachim: 68

Jeremiah: 78

Jericho: 31, 51, 52, 53, 110, 114, 115

Jerusalem: 48, 64, 67 to 70, 91 to 93, 103, 110, 115, 116, 118, 124, 137, 138, 142, 144

Jesse: 59

Jesus: 45, 60, 77, 88 to 147

Job: 76, 77

John (the apostle): 94, 95, 108, 130, 132, 141

John the Baptist: 93, 107

John the Evangelist: 89, 96

Jonah: 82 to 84

Jordan: 50, 51, 93

Joseph: 88 to 90, 92

Joseph of Arimathea: 131

Joseph (son of Jacob): 27 to 35

Joshua: 49, 50, 52 to 54

Judah: 33

Judas Iscariot: 94, 123, 126

Judas Maccabeus: 74, 75

Judea: 89, 93, 121, 137

Judith: 70, 71

L

Lazarus: 121, 122

Lebanon: 67

Luke: 88, 89

M

Mamre: 23, 24

Mark: 89

Martha: 121

Mary: 88 to 92, 96, 130

Mary Magdalene: 132

Mary (sister of Lazarus): 121

Matthew: 88, 89, 94

Mediterranean Sea: 23, 31, 89

Melchior: 91

Meshach: 79

Micah: 91

Midian: 37

Moab: 49

Mordecai: 72, 73

Moses: 36 to 38, 40 to 50, 75, 108, 120, 142

Mount Gerizim: 103

Mount Nebo: 49

Mount of Olives: 116, 126

Moreh: 23

N

Nathan: 65

Nazareth: 88, 92

Nebuchadnezzar: 48, 68, 70, 79

Nicodemus: 131

Nile: 30, 31, 36, 38

Nineveh: 23, 82, 84

Noah: 18, 20, 21, 23

O

Ozias: 70

P

Paul: 142, 144, 146, 147, 148

Persia: 69, 72, 80

Peter: 94, 107, 108, 124, 127, 132, 138, 139, 141, 146

Philip: 94

Pilate (or Pontius Pilate): 93, 128 to 130

Potiphar: 29

Q

Qantir: 36

R

Ramses II: 36
Red Sea: 31, 42
Reuben: 27
Rome: 90, 93, 128, 146, 147

S

Samaria: 103, 137
Samaritan: 110
Samson: 55, 56
Samuel: 57 to 59
Sarah: 24, 25
Satan: 76, 77
Saul: 58 to 60, 62 to 64
Shadrach: 79
Shechem: 23, 31, 54
Shiloh: 57
Simeon: 32
Simon (see Peter)
Simon the Zealot: 94
Sinai: 31, 44, 45, 48, 108
Stephen: 142, 143
Suza: 72
Sychar: 103
Syria: 146

T

Thaddeus: 94
Thomas: 94, 134
Tiberius: 93
Tigris: 23
Tyre: 67

U

Ur: 23

V

Vashti: 72

X

Xerxes: 72

Z

Zacchaeus: 114
Zedekiah: 68